ABIDING WISDOM

For Psalm-inspired prayers by
Ryan Whitaker Smith and Dan Wilt,
see **SHELTERING MERCY** *(Brazos, 2022)*
and **ENDLESS GRACE** *(Brazos, 2023).*

ABIDING WISDOM

PRAYERS INSPIRED BY THE BOOK OF PROVERBS

RYAN WHITAKER SMITH

AND DAN WILT

BrazosPress

a division of Baker Publishing Group

Grand Rapids, Michigan

Published by Brazos Press
a division of Baker Publishing Group
Grand Rapids, Michigan
BrazosPress.com

Printed in the United States of America

Library of Congress Cataloging-in-Publication Data
Names: Smith, Ryan Whitaker, 1983– author. | Wilt, Dan, author.
Title: Abiding wisdom : prayers inspired by the book of Proverbs / Ryan Whitaker Smith and Dan Wilt.
Description: Grand Rapids, Michigan : Brazos Press, a division of Baker Publishing Group, [2025]
Identifiers: LCCN 2025003644 | ISBN 9781587436239 (cloth) | ISBN 9781493452408 (ebook)
Subjects: LCSH: Bible. Proverbs—Devotional use. | Bible. Proverbs—Meditations. | Prayers.
Classification: LCC BS1465.54 .S657 2025 | DDC 242/.5—dc23/eng/20250219
LC record available at https://lccn.loc.gov/2025003644

Cover design and art: Nathan Swann

Baker Publishing Group publications use paper produced from sustainable forestry practices and postconsumer waste whenever possible.

25 26 27 28 29 30 31 7 6 5 4 3 2 1

For those who seek the God of Wisdom

May you walk the path of life,
drawn by His goodness,
astounded by His faithfulness,
renewed daily by His Spirit,
as you "grow in the grace and knowledge
of our Lord and Savior Jesus Christ" (2 Pet. 3:18)

CONTENTS

INTRODUCTION

In his first letter to the church in Corinth, the apostle Paul makes several startling claims about the nature of wisdom. He suggests that "words of eloquent wisdom" rob the Gospel message of its power—a message that appears to be the very opposite of wisdom to "those who are perishing" (1 Cor. 1:17–18). Paul paraphrases the words of the prophet Isaiah, suggesting that God is in the business of deliberately undermining and subverting what the world commonly mistakes for genuine wisdom.[1] Echoing Job, he poses the questions, "Where is the one who is wise? Where is the scribe? Where is the debater of this age?" (1:20). His queries are not merely about where a wise person may be found (if anywhere); by implication he is asking where wisdom *itself* can be found. In the words of Job, "It is hidden from the eyes of all living and concealed from the birds of the air" (Job 28:21). How, then, does one find genuine wisdom?

The Hebrew word for "wisdom," *chokmah,* speaks of a well-ordered life, a life lived in accord with God's highest

1. 1 Cor. 1:19, citing Isa. 29:14.

and best purposes. The invitation to wisdom is an invitation to bring our inner and outer lives into alignment with God's good, pleasing, and perfect will.[2] This is why, as Paul tells us in 1 Corinthians 1:24, *Christ Himself* is the ultimate manifestation of the wisdom of God.[3] He is not only the divine *Logos*, a Word of declaration eternally proclaimed by God the Father, but also the only One who could ever live in perfect alignment with the will of God. Therefore, any attempt to attain wisdom apart from Christ, "the image of the invisible God" (Col. 1:15), is an exercise in futility. As C. S. Lewis wrote, "God designed the human machine to run on Himself. He Himself is the fuel our spirits were designed to burn, or the food our spirits were designed to feed on. . . . God cannot give us happiness and peace apart from Himself, because it is not there."[4]

The treasury of sayings, riddles, maxims, and sage advice collectively known as the book of Proverbs takes seriously the idea that God "designed the human machine to run on Himself," that He is the reward of the diligent heart that seeks Him, and that He is faithful to lead us on the path of life if only we will heed His counsel to "lean not" on our "own understanding" (Prov. 3:5). In reading the book of Proverbs, we are reminded that we are not alone; others have walked the road of faith before us—in triumph and defeat—gleaning insight from the God who invites us to be fashioned and formed in His likeness, for His glory. "Behold, the fear of the Lord, that is wisdom," Job writes, "and to turn away from evil is understanding" (Job 28:28).

2. Prov. 9:10; Rom. 12:2. 3. 1 Cor. 1:24. 4. C. S. Lewis, *Mere Christianity* (Macmillan, 1952), 54.

Abiding Wisdom, like its companion volumes, *Sheltering Mercy* and *Endless Grace,* is a collection of prayers inspired by the Scriptures. These prayers are not translations or paraphrases of the text but rather *free verse renderings* intended to inspire your conversations with God. We write not as scholars or theologians but as artists and poets. While this volume is in stylistic continuity with the others, there is one difference worth noting. The format of the Psalms lent itself to our approach of one prayer per psalm. The book of Proverbs posed a unique challenge in this regard. It is more staccato in its rhythm, particularly in its latter half, where individual wisdom sayings sit alongside one another without any overt thematic connection between them. As a result, we allowed ourselves the freedom to choose specific verses or passages to use as inspiration for these prayers, without feeling the need to render each individual verse.

Our hope is that these prayers provide encouragement and insight for you, and ultimately point you to Jesus Himself, the embodiment of a life lived in accord with the Father's will—Christ, "in whom are hidden all the treasures of wisdom and knowledge" (Col. 2:3).

PROVERBS 1:2-7

ABIDING WISDOM

Lord,
wisdom begins
in knowing You[1]—
beat of Your heart,
bend of Your will,[2]
beauty of Your holiness,[3]
brightness of Your Word.[4]

To know You—
beyond mere awareness,
attention,
duty,
interest—
is my sole desire.[5]

To know You—
lost in
encounter,
presence,[6]
intimacy,[7]
reverence[8]—
is the lingering longing of my heart.

I am a child,
restless and dream-struck,
fumbling for the comfort of familiar arms.

1. Phil. 3:10. 2. Matt. 12:50. 3. Ps. 96:9. 4. Ps. 119:105. 5. Ps. 37:4. 6. Exod. 33:15–16. 7. 1 Cor. 13:12. 8. Heb. 12:28.

I am a farmer,
tamer of wild places,
tilling fallow soil in search of a hidden harvest.

I am a sailor,
adrift on the rolling dark,
seeking signs in the scattered stars.

What is wisdom,
if not the knowledge that You hold me?
What is understanding,
if not a trust that the light,
however dimly seen,
is a constellation pointing home?

But I am stiff-necked.
Slow of heart.
Loath to understand.

After all You have done for me,
I doubt Your goodness,
I question Your faithfulness.

Increase my insight!
Broaden my belief!

By Your power,
form in me
an abiding wisdom,
that I may discern
fact from fiction,
vice from virtue,
beauty from blasphemy[9]—
and so walk uprightly,

9. Phil. 1:9–11.

deal equitably,[10]
live mercifully,
run with replenishing strength
the race set before me.[11]

May I live in awe of Your kindness,
humbled by Your holiness,
strengthened by Your nearness.[12]

May I be grounded by the gravity of grace,
unintimidated by mysteries too great for me.
May my spirit be teachable,
my heart be reachable—
You desire truth in my inmost parts.[13]
May I have the mind of Christ![14]

For wisdom begins
in knowing You.

10. Lev. 19:17–18. 11. Heb. 12:1. 12. Ps. 73:28. 13. Ps. 51:6. 14. 1 Cor. 2:16.

PROVERBS 1:20–23

CROWDED HOURS

Father,
how often,
in the hurried pace of a day,
have I missed the cry of wisdom?[1]

How often,
in these crowded hours,
with every voice clamoring for advantage,
every eye vying for purchase,
have I failed to hear You?[2]
See You?

I live in a land of
desensitized souls,
surrounded by
eyes that do not see,
ears that do not hear:[3]
a world content with empty knowledge,[4]
vacuous vision.

How long will we run from the truth?
How long will we cover our wounds,
lest You heal us?

Are You not the song
humming beneath these waking moments—
a melody latent beneath the ceaseless babel;
a gentle whisper beyond

1 . Prov. 9:1–6. 2. Heb. 3:15. 3. Mark 8:18. 4. Ps. 115:4–8.

earthquake,
fire,
wind[5]—
calling us beyond these passing things?

Do You not pour Your Spirit
upon all who come to You?
The humble, You exalt.[6]
The hungry, You feed.[7]

With every rotation of the earth,
every race around the sun,
I am one step closer to Glory.[8]

I set my heart on pilgrimage,[9]
my mind on discernment,
my spirit on eternal promises.[10]

Remove my heart of stone;
give me a heart of flesh.[11]
Fill me with the peace of Your presence.[12]

Teach me, Lord,
to heed the cry of wisdom.

5. 1 Kings 19:11–12. 6. 1 Pet. 5:6. 7. Luke 1:53. 8. Ps. 63:2. 9. Ps. 84:5. 10. Eccles. 3:11. 11. Ezek. 11:19–20. 12. John 14:27.

PROVERBS 2:1–15

EMPTY VESSEL

I am an empty vessel,
waiting to be filled with Your Spirit.
I incline my ear to hear Your voice,
my heart to discern Your will,
my mind to know Your ways.[1]

How great and unsearchable
are the riches of Christ![2]

May I be a willing host to
life,
light,
perception,
vision—
beholding Your glory,
transformed into Your image,[3]
increasing in knowledge,
strengthened in power,
sharing in the inheritance of the saints.[4]

In You are hidden all the treasures of
wisdom and knowledge.[5]

When I cry out,
will You not answer me?
If I diligently seek,
will I not reap a harvest of righteousness?[6]

1. Col. 1:9–12. 2. Eph. 3:8. 3. 2 Cor. 3:18. 4. Col. 1:12. 5. Col. 2:2–3. 6. Matt. 7:7–8; Phil. 1:11.

You are the Giver of Every Perfect Gift.[7]
Imparter of Insight.
Word of Wisdom.
Lord of Life.

Through You,
image of the invisible God,
do we behold the face of God.[8]

The redeemed, You guard;
the ransomed, You shield;
the renewed, You cover:[9]
our refuge and fortress,
our eternal dwelling place.[10]

Through You we are born anew
to a living hope—
to an imperishable,
inviolate,
unfading
inheritance.[11]

By the grace of God
we will live to see the goodness of God
in the land of the living[12]—
justice and mercy
blossoming, unconstrained.

Lord Jesus,
in You all the fullness of God was pleased to dwell.[13]
Through the blood of Your cross,
You will draw all souls to Yourself.[14]

7. James 1:17. 8. Col. 1:15. 9. Zeph. 3:17. 10. Ps. 91:2. 11. 1 Pet. 1:3–4.
12. Ps. 27:13. 13. Col. 2:9–10. 14. Col. 1:19–20.

I am an empty vessel,
waiting to be filled with Your Spirit.
I incline my ear to hear Your voice,
my heart to discern Your will,
my mind to know Your ways.

PROVERBS 3:1–4

A TEACHABLE SPIRIT

Father of Wisdom,
cultivate a teachable spirit within me today.
May my heart be fertile soil,
truth taking root—
growing thirty,
sixty,
a hundredfold
what was sown.[1]

Small is the gate
and narrow is the way
that leads to life[2]—

I have counted all things as loss
for the joy of knowing You.[3]

Heavy is the weight of the cross,
the affliction of the flesh,
these trials and tribulations,
this daily dying[4]—

Your yoke is easy;
Your burden is light.[5]

Though I am fickle,
forgetful,
faithless,
You are unshakable,

1. Matt. 13:23. 2. Matt. 7:13–14. 3. Phil. 3:8. 4. Luke 9:23. 5. Matt. 11:30.

unmovable,
unchangeable.[6]

The same yesterday,
today,
forever.[7]

When my love is dim,
Yours grows more radiant still.
When sin plagues me,
Your mercy proves more than enough.

My grace is sufficient for You.
My power is made perfect in weakness.[8]

When my heart is
unteachable,
unreachable,
resistant to humility,
lead me to repentance.

In Your mercy,
turn Your face to me:
You, the Potter;
I, the clay.[9]

Set me, O Lord,
between the rock
and the hard place—
that I might depend upon You,
abandoning my stubbornness,
sacrificing my self-sufficiency.

6. James 1:17. 7. Heb. 13:8. 8. 2 Cor. 12:9. 9. Isa. 64:8.

You search me,
know me,
find me.[10]
May pride not keep me from the knowledge of
Your Way,
Your Truth,
Your Life.[11]

In the midst of conflict,
teach me to honor my opponent
as a fellow image bearer,
repaying evil with good.[12]

Teach me to discern the times,[13]
make peace with transience,
acknowledge my own mortality.

You alone hold eternity in Your hands.
You alone dwell in unapproachable light.[14]

When my flesh has been destroyed,
I will see You,[15]
know You,
as I have been seen,
known.

Lord, have mercy.
Christ, have mercy.[16]

Give me a heart to know You.
A will to follow You.
Ears to hear You.
Eyes to see You.[17]

10. Ps. 139:23. 11. John 14:6. 12. Rom. 12:17–21. 13. Ps. 39:4. 14. 1 Tim. 6:16.
15. Job 19.26. 16. Derived from the Kyrie Prayer of liturgical tradition.
17. Matt. 13:16.

May I never forget
who You are;
who I am in You.

Clothe me in Your salvation,[18]
write Your will upon my mind,
Your Word upon my heart,
that blessing upon blessing
would follow me
as I follow You.

Father of Wisdom,
cultivate a teachable spirit within me today.
May my heart be fertile soil,
truth taking root—
growing thirty,
sixty,
a hundredfold
what was sown.

18. Isa. 61:10.

PROVERBS 3:5–10

THE MIND OF CHRIST

Trust

Lord,
so often I am at the mercy
of what I can
see,
feel,
touch—
while the assurance of hope[1]
eludes me.

Lay waste to my pride.
Humble my wisdom.
Give me the mind of Christ.[2]

Understanding

When I lean upon my own
thoughts,
perceptions,
comprehensions—
as if I could discern
the indiscernible—
save me from the tyranny
of self-lordship;
lead me on the path to life.

I rest in Your presence.
I yield to Your grace.
May Your favor rest upon me.[3]

1. Heb. 11:1. 2. 1 Cor. 2:16. 3. Deut. 7:9.

Acknowledgment

If I fail to see You,
succumb to blindness,
stumble down the paths of the dead,
guide me back from ruin:
Shepherd,[4]
Comforter,[5]
Friend[6]—
Joyful Presence,
Enduring Pleasure.[7]

Who is like You, Lord?[8]
Exalted above the heavens,[9]
Savior of all who call upon Your name?[10]

Direction

To walk with You,
to follow in Your steps,
is life,
peace,
joy—
a level ground,
a lamp-lit way[11]—
deliverance from fear,
evil,
ceaseless wandering.

I cannot escape You
in heaven's heights
or earth's depths.[12]

4. John 10:14–15. 5. John 14:26. 6. John 15:15. 7. Ps. 16:11. 8. Exod. 15:11. 9. Ps. 57:5. 10. Rom. 10:13. 11. Ps. 119:105. 12. Ps. 139:7–8.

Healing

In reverence I will live:
whole,
healed,
healing,
strengthened by
reason,
goodness,
kindness.

You who began a good work in me
will bring it to completion
at the day of Christ Jesus.[13]

Honor

In all my ways I will honor You,
acknowledge You,[14]
magnify You.[15]
Grant me the faith to trust,
to submit my understanding
to the leading of Your Spirit,
to follow You to Kingdom Come.

May my life be a testimony
to the words You have spoken over me:
I have the mind of Christ.[16]

Amen.

13. Phil. 1:6. 14. Prov. 3:6. 15. Ps. 34:3. 16. 1 Cor. 2:16.

PROVERBS 3:13–18

WISDOM SEEKER

Lord God,
I do not ask for
pleasure,
comfort,
wealth,
recognition.
I do not seek
transient pleasures
or momentary fame.

My deepest desire,
the fervent yearning of my soul,
is to see as You see,
love as You love:
to walk in the way of wisdom.

To follow You
is life.
To rest in You
is peace.[1]
To worship You
is joy.

Your counsel is my comfort,
Your guidance my grounding.

I am a wisdom seeker,
digging in the dirt
in search of buried treasure,[2]

1. John 14:27. 2. Matt. 13:44.

plumbing the ocean deep
to find a pearl of great price.[3]

Are You not the reward of all who diligently seek You?
Do You not give more than we can ask or imagine?[4]

In my poverty,
Your presence makes me rich.
In my brokenness,
Your mercy makes me whole.

Who am I, Lord,
that You,
God of Wisdom,[5]
would teach me Your ways?
That Your hand would reach for me
as I reach for You?[6]

I am a wisdom seeker,
brushing close with
death,
suffering,
failure,
rising to
life,
healing,
strength—
growing in the knowledge of Christ,
that I may know as I am known,
see as I am seen.[7]

At the end of my days,
when my flesh grows weak
and my eyes grow dim,

3. Matt. 13:45. 4. Eph. 3:20. 5. Rom. 16:27. 6. James 4:8. 7. 1 John 3:2.

what heritage would I leave behind
but to be known as
beloved of God,
disciple of Christ,
one who pursued truth,
loved goodness,
fell upon mercy?

For I have eaten of the Tree of Life
and found life everlasting.[8]

8. Rom. 6:22.

PROVERBS 3:19–27

NEW MERCIES

Father,
as I step into the unknown of a new day—
opening heart and hands
to receive Your mercies,
which are new[1]
as the day is new—
may the wisdom that is fear of You[2]
anoint my eyes.
May I see not what is
but perhaps,
by holy possibility,
what could be,
should be.[3]

May Your hand
guide me with indiscernible grace—
a gentle whisper,
a wind at the back—
that I may not stray
like the wandering sheep I am[4]
but remain
steadfast,
foot-sure,
on the path of life.[5]

Left to my own sense,
will I not digress?

1. Lam. 3:22–23. 2. Ps. 111:10. 3. Eph. 1:17–18. 4. Isa. 53:6. 5. Ps. 16:11.

Stumble into God-knows-what
in God-knows-where?
Only to kick the dirt,
pound my fists,
cry for rescue?
(I am nothing if not predictable.)

And You?
You would come again—
a lantern swinging in the dark.
Gently:
Come along, now;
come home.[6]

If I am with You,
You with me,
should I not be
zealous in faith,
bold in confidence,
fearing nothing?[7]
(I am crippled with fear.)

If You brood above me,
singing over all my chaos—
if I am safe in Your arms—
should rest not follow me?
The deep shalom of God
enveloping,
enfolding,
bringing unreasonable peace,
sleep so deep and pure
that only the sun can sing me awake?
(Peace eludes me. Sleep shuns me.)

6. John 14:23. 7. Phil. 4:6.

Perhaps,
in the end,
You are teaching me,
through all this daily dying,
to let go.

Grant me grace
to trust that You are not only with me
but for me;[8]
that You not only love me
but live in me;[9]
that I am—
as the day is,
as the dew is,
as Your mercies are—
new.[10]

8. Rom. 8:31. 9. Col. 1:27. 10. 2 Cor. 5:17.

PROVERBS 3:31–33

SHEPHERD OF MY SOUL

Shepherd of My Soul,[1]
I come to You today,
discontent,
dissatisfied,
disillusioned.

Lord, Jesus Christ,
have mercy on me,
a sinner.[2]

Envy, once again,
has seized my heart,[3]
and I—
slow to
resist,
restrain,
retreat—
have been led astray.

Wed to covetousness,[4]
bound to lust,[5]
given over to hate,[6]
I am lured,
enticed,
dragged down the paths of the dead.[7]

Lord, Jesus Christ,
have mercy on me,
a sinner.

1. Ps. 23:1; 1 Pet. 2:25. 2. Derived from the Jesus Prayer of liturgical tradition. 3. Titus 3:3–7. 4. Mark 7:21–23. 5. Rom. 1:24. 6. Titus 3:3. 7. Prov. 14:12.

When my heart languishes,
when my soul yearns for liberation,
lead me to the rock that is higher than I,[8]
above noise and clamor,
cacophonous cursing,
disordered desire.[9]

Draw my eyes to the heights,
for You are my help:[10]
Shepherd of My Soul.

Lead me on paths of righteousness,
for the sake of Your name.
Enlighten this darkness.
Wrest me from ruin.[11]

At every moment I am in danger of stumbling—
save me, Lord!
The wicked flounder in darkness,
but those who know Your voice
follow You
and find rest for their souls.

When I am blind to the truth, enlighten my eyes.
Remind me of the hope to which I am called,
the glorious inheritance of the saints.[12]

May I feed in pastures green,[13]
flourish by rushing waters—
an oak of righteousness
for the display of Your glory.[14]

By Your grace,
may I dwell in the house of the Lord
forever.[15]

8. Ps. 61:1–2. 9. Inspired by Augustine, *Confessions* 4.10.15.
10. Ps. 121:1–2. 11. Ps. 23:4. 12. Eph. 1:18. 13. Ps. 23:2. 14. Isa. 61:3.
15. Ps. 23:6.

PROVERBS 4:14–19

LIGHT ETERNAL

Light Eternal,
lamp upon the path of life,[1]
illumine my steps.[2]

Lord,
keep me on the narrow way—
for wide is the road descending in darkness:
a spiraling march to the grave.[3]

May my feet be steady,
my eyes centered,
my heart pure.

May I prove myself to be
a faithful follower,
a loyal co-laborer
to those who walk beside me.

Fill me with Your Spirit, Lord,
until my hunger for sin is starved
and all darkness in me is light.[4]

The godless feast on wickedness,
grow sick with selfish greed.
Gluttonous in lust,
they are full but never satisfied—
while at Your right hand are
pleasures forevermore.[5]

1. Ps. 16:11. 2. Ps. 119:105. 3. Matt. 7:13–14. 4. Luke 11:36. 5. Ps. 16:11.

Light Eternal,
lamp upon the path of life,
illumine my steps.

May my life be a testimony of
wisdom heeded,
holiness embodied,
eternity envisioned[6]—
as I walk in the light of
those who have gone before me,
seeking to light the way for those who follow behind—
my path a witness to
lessons learned,
insight acquired,
counsel embraced;
for the darkness is
ever-increasing,
ever-pursuing,
hungry to swallow every
hope,
dream,
desire.

Deliver me, Lord.

For those who walk in step with You,
the light is stronger still—
an unstoppable,
inextinguishable
brilliance.

Light Eternal,
lamp upon the path of life,
illumine my steps.

6. Eccles. 3:11.

PROVERBS 4:23–27

SPRING OF LIFE

Spring of Life,
flow from my heart today.[1]
Living Waters, burst forth,
unhindered by
sin,
fear,
shame;
unrestrained by
cowardice,
resistance,
selfish desire.[2]

Rush through this dry-bone valley,
drawing life from the dust[3]—
a stalk,
a petal,
a twisting vine
becomes a
flowering,
blossoming
abundance.[4]

Course in me
and through me—
to irrigate,
invigorate,
rejuvenate
the weak and wounded souls about me.

1. Luke 6:45. 2. Rom. 6:12. 3. Matt. 11:4–5. 4. Ps. 65:9–10.

Sanctify this sin-struck tongue,
that all my words would bless rather than curse,
consecrate rather than desecrate.

Swing wide my gates,[5]
that this rushing cataract of joy
might cascade in continual communion.

Let me gaze upon Your beauty,
that these shame-marred eyes
would be fixed in unwavering devotion to You:
Author.
Perfector.[6]
Wondrous Well of Living Water.[7]

May I resist the downward pitch of sin,
the casual slide to ruin.

Strengthen me,
that all my steps may be stable,
my course steady,
my intentions pure.

Spring of Life,
flow from my heart today.
Living Waters, burst forth!

5. Ps. 24:7–10. 6. Heb. 12:1–2. 7. John 7:38.

PROVERBS 5:3–6, 15–20

THE GIFTS YOU GIVE

Lord God,
by the power of Your Spirit,
may I resist temptation,
embrace contentment,
walk in integrity.

In a world of wayward passion,
every day brings new seductions:
fleeting promises of pleasure,
window shopping for the covetous,
a feast for famished eyes.

At every turn,
I am accosted by lying voices,
a chorus of idolatry,
beguiling the weary and weak-willed.

Like a lamb led to the slaughter,
I have been
tempted,
persuaded,
gratified,
disgraced.

I do not do what I want.
I do the very thing I hate.[1]
Have mercy on me, Lord.

1. Rom. 7:15.

May the gifts You give
be enough for me.[2]
May I be satisfied,
content,
grateful.

As for me and my house,
may we serve You.[3]
May we walk with integrity of heart,
setting nothing before our eyes that is worthless,
knowing nothing of evil.[4]

By the power of the Holy Spirit,
may we abound in hope[5]—
for all Your ways
are life and peace.

May I tend to Your gifts[6]
with gladness of heart—
recognizing limitation,
resisting excess,
growing in grace,
venturing deeper and deeper
into the depths of Your love.[7]

The enemy of my soul seeks to
steal,
kill,
destroy—
twisting truth,
distorting the good and perfect gifts
of Your hand.

2. James 1:17. 3. Josh. 24:15. 4. Ps. 101:2–4. 5. Rom. 15:13. 6. James 1:17.
7. Ps. 42:7.

May I resist him,
firm in faith,[8]
that he might flee from me.
May I draw near to You,
that You would draw near to me.[9]

Teach me, O Lord,
to find joy where You have planted me:
in plenty,
in hunger,
in prosperity,
in need.[10]

Teach me, O Lord,
not to covet that which is not mine
but to thrive in the land of my possession,
woven in intimate delight
into a tapestry of Your making.

Lord God,
by the power of Your Spirit,
may I resist temptation,
embrace contentment,
walk in integrity.

Amen.

8. 1 Pet. 5:9. 9. James 4:7. 10. Phil. 4:11–12.

PROVERBS 6:20–23

ANCIENT PATHS

Lord,
I thank You that I am not
a solitary traveler on the road of faith.
The path I tread is one of
inherited insight,
embodied knowledge,
generational faithfulness.

May I receive with
meekness and humility
the counsel of the past.
May it
clothe me,
nourish me,
guide me,
caution me.

I am not
self-existent,
self-sufficient,
self-sustained.
I am at the mercy of
Your breath
to revive me,
Your provision
to uphold me,
Your revelation
to direct me.

Is it not You who speaks through the ages, Lord?
Who gives counsel
in the whispers of the past?
Who speaks in the night,
in the stirring of the heart?[1]

Who am I,
that such
grace and kindness
should follow me,
that such favor should
precede and succeed me?[2]

May I not be like those who scorn
the old ways,
who look with contempt
upon the aged.

May I resist
the temptations of
the new and the novel,
the condescending pride
of this passing age.

May I be one who follows
the Ancient Paths,[3]
in step with
the Ancient of Days,
one who practices patient obedience,
who inquires of bygone ages.[4]

For You declare the end from the beginning.[5]
You are the Alpha.
The Omega.[6]

1. Ps. 16:7–8. 2. Ps. 23:6. 3. Jer. 6:16. 4. Job 8:8. 5. Isa. 46:10. 6. Rev. 22:13.

To You, one day is as a thousand years,
a thousand years as one day.[7]

In joy,
may I remember those who have
suffered before me.
In pain,
may I remember those who have
triumphed before me.
In darkness,
may I be guided by the light
of generations past.

For I am surrounded by a cloud of witnesses
to the faithfulness of God.
May I run with endurance
the race set before me,[8]
that those to come
would follow in my steps.

Amen.

7. 2 Pet. 3:8 8. Heb. 12:1.

PROVERBS 7:1-4

WORD DIVINE

Word Divine[1]—
God of God,
Light of Light,
Lord Jesus Christ[2]—
I follow You.

You are the Word of Reason[3]
in the midst of sparring tongues—
a severing clarity that
pierces,
humbles,
discerns
the thoughts
and intentions
of the heart.[4]

You are the Word of Life
in the midst of death and darkness—
resurrection breath
that defies the grave,
raises flesh
and bone
and sinew
from the dust.

Bread of Life.
Living Water.
Word Made Flesh.

1. John 1:1, 14. 2. Inspired by the words of the Nicene Creed. 3. Isa. 1:18.
4. Heb. 4:12.

Your precepts
are nourishment
to my soul.

Your Word-Shaped World
proclaims Your goodness.
You are
Lord of the Seas.[5]
Master of Wild Places.[6]
King of the Heavens.
Revelatory Vision.
God with Us.[7]

Worship the Lord,
O my soul!
Forget not all His benefits![8]
Ever keep His ways!

Word Divine—
God of God,
Light of Light,
Lord Jesus Christ—
I follow You.

5. Mark 4:35–41. 6. Ps. 24:1. 7. Matt. 1:23. 8. Ps. 103:2.

PROVERBS 8:1–11

THE VOICE OF WISDOM

Lord God,
give me the ears to hear
the voice of Wisdom.
In season,
out of season,
in silence,
storm,
morning,
evening,
waking moments,
dreaming dark,
in the company of friends,
in the presence of enemies—
may I listen,
heed,
obey.

I seek not the wisdom of this age,
which is doomed to pass away,
but the hidden Wisdom of God—
ordained before
all ages,
all peoples,
all kingdoms[1]—
timeless truth proclaimed across time.

1. 1 Cor. 2:4–7.

To the
frightened,
fearful,
faint of heart;
to the
rebel,
drifter,
seeker;
to the
insolent,
arrogant,
self-absorbed;
to the sick,
dying,
languishing;
to the sinner,
saint,
doubter—
all with ears to hear
will hear.[2]

To those who ask,
it will be given.
For those who knock,
the door will be opened to them.[3]

For never is the truth
not proclaimed.
Never does Wisdom
cease to speak.

2. Matt. 11:15. 3. Matt. 7:7–8.

The Logos of God is
living,
active,
piercing to the division
of soul and spirit.[4]

O my soul,
praise,
honor,
extol
the King of Heaven—
His works are right,
His ways are just,
and those who walk in pride
He is faithful to humble.[5]

Lord,
give me the ears to hear
the voice of Wisdom—
to clothe myself in humility,[6]
to seek truth over riches,
knowledge over pleasure,
holiness over comfort.

Amen.

4. Heb. 4:12. 5. Dan. 4:37. 6. 1 Pet. 5:5.

PROVERBS 8:22-31

YOU WERE THERE

Ancient Wisdom,
decreed before time began,
guide me in the
Way of Life.

Before the world
was spun into being,
before the Spirit of God
hovered over the waters,[1]
You were there.

Before the cerulean vault of the sky
was stretched east to west,[2]
before the sea
surged with the carnival of the deep,[3]
You were there.

Before man was formed from the dust,
before inspiriting breath filled his lungs,[4]
You were there.

Before the first lie,
before the first trespass,
before the pall of death
fell on all God-created things,[5]
You were there.

Even in our waywardness,
our self-sabotage,

1. Gen. 1:2. 2. Gen. 1:6. 3. Gen. 1:20–22. 4. Gen. 2:7. 5. Gen. 3:1–24.

our hereditary digression,
You speak, still.

Wisdom Eternal,
Manifest Truth,
Sacred Revelation:
who am I,
that I should be granted to know
the hidden ways of God?[6]

I,
sin-bent,
trouble-prone,
slow to learn,
hesitant to change—
You have raised from death to life,[7]
called a New Creation,[8]
granted the mind of Christ.[9]

Everlasting promise,
endless grace,
eternal insight
are mine by the power of Your Spirit.[10]

Rejoice, Wisdom Eternal,
in the majesty of it all!

Rejoice, Wisdom Eternal,
in my heart made whole!

Rejoice, Wisdom Eternal,
in the story of redemption!

6. Prov. 25:2. 7. Rom. 6:4. 8. 2 Cor. 5:17. 9. 1 Cor. 2:16. 10. Eph. 3:16–21.

May all creation sing praises,
all created things
wonder at Your decrees![11]

As it was in the beginning,
is now, and ever shall be,
world without end.[12]

Ancient Wisdom,
decreed before time began,
guide me in the
Way of Life.

Amen.

11. Ps. 119:129–30. 12. Derived from the *Gloria Patri* (*Glory Be to the Father*) doxology of liturgical tradition.

PROVERBS 9:1–6

THE HOUSE OF WISDOM

Lead me,
my Lord and God,
to the House of Wisdom,[1]
enshrined upon a hill called "Holy,"[2]
the resting place of all who diligently seek Your face.

Her foundations are Truth,[3]
her pillars are Beauty,[4]
her walls are Goodness.[5]

Grace upon grace
is granted to all who enter her doors,
who heed her call:

"Turn from empty things,
from profitless idols,
from sin and sorrow—
enter here,
and know the joy of the Lord."

Cleansing waters flow
to restore the broken will
and heavy heart.[6]

A bountiful table is set—
rich food
and hearty drink

1. Prov. 9:1. 2. Ryan Whitaker Smith and Dan Wilt, *Sheltering Mercy: Prayers Inspired by the Psalms* (Brazos, 2022), 44. 3. John 17:17. 4. Phil. 4:8. 5. Ps. 86:5. 6. John 14:1.

to refresh the weary,
invigorate the sojourning soul.

How my soul longs,
my flesh faints
for the courts of the Lord![7]

In Your grace,
You have prepared a table for me[8]
at the feast of the redeemed:
clothed me in righteousness,
seated me in a place of honor,
a joy too wonderful for me.[9]

You have anointed my head with oil;
my cup overflows:[10]
fed me with mercy,
led me with kindness,
sustained me with a love
unfailing and true.

You have set Your goodness to follow me
all the days of my life:[11]
breathed life into my spirit,
brought gladness into my soul,
guided me in right paths
for the sake of Your name.[12]

I will dwell in Your house,
forever.[13]

Lead me,
my Lord and God,

7. Ps. 84:10. 8. Ps. 23:5. 9. Ps. 139:6. 10. Ps. 23:5. 11. Ps. 23:6. 12. Ps. 23:3. 13. Ps. 23:6.

to the House of Wisdom,
enshrined upon a hill called "Holy,"
the resting place of all who diligently seek Your face.

Amen.

PROVERBS 9:7–12

SLOW OBEDIENCE

May I be teachable, Lord.

Cultivate a childlike spirit within me[1]*—*
that I may learn to listen,
by loving instruction
and caring correction—
inclining my ear to counsel,[2]
my heart to direction.

I have seen others
filled with the pride of life:[3]
contemptuous,
resentful,
insisting on their own way.

They refuse the guidance of friends,
scorn the words of the wise,[4]
shun all that might heal them.

Save me from such deceptions, Lord,
from the bondage of arrogance,
the slavery of self-centeredness.[5]
May I sit at the feet of
souls wiser than I,
receptive to the
slow work of Your Spirit.

This is my heart's desire:
to rightly discern

1. Matt. 18:3; Mark 10:15. 2. Prov. 5:1. 3. 1 John 2:16. 4. Prov. 12:15. 5. Phil. 3:19.

truth from falsehood,
revelation from imagination,
the leading of Your Spirit
from the leaning of my flesh.

For the unenlightened,
wisdom is a passing phrase:
in one ear,
out the other.
They are sproutless seeds,[6]
a house built upon sand.[7]

As for me,
may my heart be good ground, Lord,
fruitful soil where truth might take root.

May the walls of my soul be secure,
built upon the rock,
a shield to the four winds.[8]

In the company of the wise,[9]
I am strong,
my soul rich with wealth
that neither moth nor rust destroys;[10]
joy of
heart,
mind,
strength[11]
overflowing.

Clothe me in Christ.[12]
Robe me in righteousness—
for You are the vine,
I the branch,[13]

6. Matt. 13:3–8. 7. Matt. 7:26. 8. Matt. 7:24–25. 9. Prov. 15:31. 10. Matt. 6:20. 11. Deut. 6:5. 12. Rom. 13:14. 13. John 15:5.

growing in slow obedience
in flesh and spirit;
shielded from winter's bite,
nourished by Your countless mercies.

Cultivate a childlike spirit in me—
that I may learn to listen,
by loving instruction
and caring correction—
inclining my ear to counsel,
my heart to direction.

Amen.

PROVERBS 10:2–9

I COUNT ALL AS LOSS

Lord Jesus,
for the joy of knowing You,[1]
I count all as loss.[2]

I have gathered about me
comforts,
pleasures,
empty promises.

I have wandered down the wide way,[3]
indulging in lust of
flesh,
eyes,
pride,
life,[4]
led astray
by my own desire.

Precious few walk Your way,[5]
follow the call of God
down the cruciform path
to life abundant.[6]

Lead me in the path of life, Lord.

In my hunger,
You feed me.
In my lostness,
You guide me.

1. Phil. 3:10–11. 2. Phil. 3:7–8. 3. Matt. 7:13. 4. 1 John 2:16. 5. Ps. 89:15. 6. John 10:10.

In Your strength,
may I strive to
do all things well,
finish all things well,
until all things are well.

May I be diligent to plant,
that I may bountifully reap.[7]
May I work heartily as for You,
that favor would follow me
as I follow You[8]—
mercy and goodness chasing me
all the days of my life.[9]

May my tongue praise You,
my lips honor You,
my heart yearn for You,
my flesh faint for You.[10]

May I be a living witness
to the nearness of God,
an embodied testament of communion.

You, my Provider.
You, my Sustainer.
You, Hope of My Heart.
You, Joy of My Soul.

May I follow in the steps of the saints:
sitting at Your feet,[11]
receiving Your counsel,
running with endurance,[12]
entering the joy of my Master.

7. James 3:18. 8. Prov. 10:6. 9. Ps. 23:6. 10. Ps. 63:1. 11. Luke 10:38–42. 12. Heb. 12:1–2.

Lord Jesus,
for the sake of knowing You,
I count all as loss.

PROVERBS 10:11–14, 17–21

INSTRUMENT OF BLESSING

Father,
caught up in controversy
and confrontation,
we have lost our ability to bless,
instead we only curse.[1]

Hatred stirs our anger.
Prejudice stokes our fear.
We are fluent in blasphemy.

Lord,
have mercy.
Forgive me,
a sinner.[2]

Love is the way:[3]
to speak,
act,
touch
a world in need of healing.

Love is the way:
to confront,
challenge,
resist
a world in need of wisdom.

Love is the way:
to strengthen,

1. Rom. 12:14. 2. Derived from the Jesus Prayer of liturgical tradition.
3. 1 Cor. 14:1.

refresh,
renew
a world in need of revival.

Without love,
I am nothing.[4]

In the tongue is the power
of life
and death.[5]
With our words we are
justified
or condemned.[6]

Forgive me, Lord,
for damning
rather than hallowing,
grumbling
rather than praising,
for allowing bitterness
and rancor
to take residence in me.

May love and faithfulness be wed[7]
in my spirit;
may those who oppose me
see the fruit of my life—
integrity,
dignity,
sound speech—
and have nothing to say against me.

May my tongue
be an instrument of

4. 1 Cor. 13:1–13. 5. Prov. 18:21. 6. Matt. 12:33–37. 7. Ps. 85:10.

blessing,
healing,
peace.

May I honor You
with the words of my mouth
and the meditation of my heart.[8]

Amen.

8. Ps. 19:14.

PROVERBS 11:1–8

MERCIFUL GOD

Merciful God,
here I am again—
stalked by pride:
a relentless,
malicious
presence,
pledging fleeting pleasures
and empty promises.

With humiliating frequency
I have run into the arms of trouble,
a moth to a flame,
only to fall
time and again
upon Your grace.[1]

In my brokenness,
rebuild me.
In my waywardness,
reorient me.
In my lawlessness,
reaffirm me.

Grant me the strength to stand against
every temptation,
every lie,
every scheme of the accuser.[2]

1. 2 Cor. 12:9. 2. Eph. 6:13.

May worship be my defense,
integrity my rear guard.
May nothing stand against
Your purposes in me.
May every enemy
submit to Your lordship.[3]

I will not be like those who fill
earthly storehouses
with temporary treasures,[4]
only to be impoverished in eternity.

Rather,
I will pursue
love,
joy,
peace,
patience,
kindness,
goodness,
faithfulness,
gentleness,
self-control[5]—
that I may have treasure in heaven
and walk in Your fullness.

Merciful God,
deliver me!

Merciful God,
sustain me!

Merciful God,
direct me!

3. Phil. 2:9–11. 4. Matt. 6:20. 5. Gal. 5:22–23.

Set my course, Lord.
Lead me in the Way of Life.[6]

Amen.

6. Ps. 16:11.

PROVERBS 11:23–28, 30

CHEERFUL GIVER

Father God,
grant me the grace
of the cheerful giver:[1]
to meet a need
by Your great provision,
drawing from the storehouses of Your mercy—
for the weak,
the poor,
the needy.[2]

I will not hoard wealth
for temporal gain,
passing pleasures,
momentary comforts.

As You have given generously,
I will give generously:
of my time,
resources,
strength—
for where my treasure is,
there my heart is also.[3]

There is blessing in giving:
to meet a need
out of the bounty of Your abundance,
to fill the hungry with good things.[4]

1. 2 Cor. 9:7. 2. Prov. 28:27. 3. Luke 12:34. 4. Ps. 107:9.

There is blessing in receiving:
to humbly accept Your grace
through the kindness of others.

Gratitude sows seeds of
peace in the mind
and
hope in the heart.

Blessed are those who give cheerfully
without compulsion,
who seek every opportunity to show charity—
for they will gain a crown of righteousness.[5]

As the saints before me were sent to those in need,
hearts burning with the fire of mission—
no silver or gold to give,
but moved by a love to
heal the sick
and raise the dead—
send me, Lord.

May I love as I have been loved.[6]

When I withhold mercy,
stifle compassion,
cling to mammon,[7]
I am a dammed stream,
a well filled with stones.

Freely I have received.
Freely I will give.[8]

None who believes in You
will ever go hungry—

5. 2 Tim. 4:8. 6. John 13:34. 7. Matt. 6:24. 8. Matt. 10:8.

for You are the Bread of Life.[9]
None who comes to You
will ever go thirsty—
for You are the Water of Life.[10]

As You laid down Your life for me,
may I lay down my life for others.[11]

Generous Provider,
grant me the grace
of the cheerful giver.

Amen.

9. John 6:35. 10. John 6:55. 11. John 15:13.

PROVERBS 12:1, 3, 7

THE STORY OF YOUR TELLING

Father,
the story of my life
is a story of Your telling.

Moments perceived
and unperceived,
paths taken
and neglected,
devastating failure,
unexpected grace,
step by step,
breath by breath—
You are present in it all.

What an unfathomable mystery,
this dance of human will
and divine sovereignty;
a lifetime's meditation
could not unravel it.

May I trust in the story of Your telling,
walk in confidence and strength,
in the sure knowledge of
who You are,
who I am—
for You are trustworthy and true;

in You I go from strength to strength;[1]
my mourning becomes dancing,
my sorrow gives way to joy.[2]

I will trust in the sure hand of God.

I have had enough of my own understanding,
the confidence of my own experience;[3]
I am painfully aware of the limits of my knowledge.

Grant that I may be like a child, Lord:[4]
innocence renewed,
eyes wide with wonder.

May my spirit be teachable.

Those who are confident in their own strength,
who resist truth's embrace,
content with the wisdom of this age,
lose their footing,
tumble into ruin.

Self-absorbed,
self-seeking,
they vanish into their own narratives,
every story beginning and ending with themselves.

Better is one day in Your house
than a thousand elsewhere.[5]

Father,
the story of my life
is a story of Your telling.

May I trust that at the end of my days,
You will bring this tale to its fitting end;

1. Ps. 84:7. 2. Ps. 30:11. 3. Prov. 28:11. 4. Mark 10:15. 5. Ps. 84:10.

that all pain will be redeemed,
all failure righted,
all virtue rewarded,
all riddles unraveled—
as I behold You face to face[6]
and dwell with You forever.[7]

Amen.

6. 1 Cor. 13:12. 7. Ps. 23:6.

PROVERBS 12:25

A GOOD WORD

Lord,
it is a heavy load that
burdens the heart,
depresses the mind,
delivers the soul to
sorrow,
anxiety,
despair.[1]

Like a stone sunk in the sea,
my spirit descends
in darkness,[2]
lost in the caverns of the deep.

When all seems lost,
Your Good Word comes—
a revelatory kindness in
deed,
touch,
whisper,
song.

If I make my bed in the depths,
You are there.[3]

Your Good Word is healing
to the suffering soul,
salve to the wounded spirit.

1. John 14:1. 2. Ps. 139:7. 3. Ps. 139:8.

Teach me, Lord,
to keep Your Word
hidden in my heart[4]—
that when desolation strikes,
when despair threatens to steal my joy,
I would call to mind Your promises,[5]
take comfort in Your presence.[6]

In good time,
Your Good Word comes—
to speak deliverance,
execute justice,
rekindle hope,
reignite passion.

For Your Word does not return void,
but seeds and sprouts
in the ground of Your planting,
accomplishing all Your purposes.[7]

Amen.

4. Ps. 119:11. 5. Ps. 119:48. 6. 2 Cor. 1:3. 7. Isa. 55:10–11.

PROVERBS 13:12, 14, 19

FOUNTAINS OF LIFE

Fountains of life
water the wide world
with the wisdom of God—
springs of living water
flowing from the hearts of the saints[1]
for the flourishing of the earth.

Let justice roll like a river!
Righteousness like a mighty stream![2]

Fountains of life
water the weary world
with Hope, Light, Life—
streams of mercy
flowing from the outpouring of the Spirit
for the healing of the nations.[3]

You will pour water on the thirsty land!
Streams on the dry ground![4]

Fountains of life
water the waiting world
with gifts of vision and rapture—
rivers of eternal rest
flowing from the city of God
for the renewal of creation.[5]

In good time,
this broken earth

1. John 4:13–14. 2. Amos 5:24. 3. Rev. 22:1–2. 4. Isa. 44:3. 5. Rev. 21:5.

will be filled with Your knowledge
as the waters cover the sea.[6]

Your river will wind through
the streets of Your eternal city,
beneath the branches of the Tree of Life,
given for the healing of the nations[7]—
a river whose streams make glad the city of God,[8]
the holy place where You will dwell with us.[9]

Come!
You declare.
All who are thirsty,
all who are weary,
all who are destitute,[10]
come and drink of the Water of Life
and thirst no more.[11]

Amen.

6. Hab. 2:14. 7. Rev. 22:2. 8. Ps. 46:4. 9. Rev. 21:3. 10. Isa. 55:1. 11. John 4:14.

PROVERBS 14:12, 16–18

STEADFAST

Father,
You are Light,
in whom there is no shadow,
no variation,
no change.[1]

You have set before us
life
and death,
the way of consecration
and desecration.
In Your mercy,
You have called us to
life inexhaustible,
overflowing,
unending.[2]

Help me, Lord,
to fix my eyes upon Your face,
my feet upon Your way[3]—
that I may be steadfast,
unwavering,
turning not to the right
or to the left.[4]

The wayward soul strays,
swayed by the passions of the flesh,

1. James 1:17. 2. John 10:10. 3. Jude 1:24–25. 4. Prov. 4:27.

by pride and ambition,[5]
lust and envy.

Those who live by the flesh
set their minds on the things of the flesh.[6]

Have I not also been reckless?
Am I not also prone to leave the God I love?[7]

Extend Your mercy to me, Lord!
Intervene for me,
that I might walk in freedom
and fullness of joy.[8]

Restore me,
that I might forget what lies behind
and press on toward what is ahead.[9]

For to set the mind on the flesh is death,
but to set the mind on the Spirit
is life and peace.[10]

May anger and resentment
be far from me.
May I resist the enemy,
that he would flee from me.[11]

For I have set my heart on You, O Lord,[12]
and I will not be moved.[13]

I choose the path of life,[14]
running with endurance
the race set before me,
eyes fixed on You,

5. Gal. 5:19–21. 6. Col. 3:2. 7. Inspired by a line from the hymn "Come, Thou Fount of Every Blessing" (1758) by Robert Robinson. 8. Ps. 16:11. 9. Phil. 3:14. 10. Rom. 8:6. 11. James 4:7. 12. Ps. 119:30. 13. Ps. 16:8. 14. Ps. 16:11.

who endured the cross
for the joy
of New Creation dawning:[15]
the revealing of the children of God.[16]

Amen.

15. Heb. 12:1–2. 16. Rom. 8:19.

PROVERBS 14:26-27

IN HIGHEST REGARD

In highest regard
I hold You, Lord—
Master,
Redeemer,[1]
Friend.[2]

I esteem Your Way,
Your Truth,
Your Life[3]
above all else.

With reverent awe
I consider Your works—
creation born from Your breath,
humankind spun from the dust;
the wild,
teeming,
miraculous
dance of life;
the relentless pursuit of grace.

Though I am poor and needy,
You make Your home with me.
I walk in confident hope—
not in my own strength
but because of Your abiding presence.[4]

My heart is steadfast, O God,[5]
resisting the sway of sin,

1. Ps. 19:14. 2. John 15:15. 3. John 14:6. 4. Matt. 1:23. 5. Ps. 108:1.

the pull of lesser things.
May I live as one reborn:[6]
a New Creation in Christ.[7]

I have forsaken the ways of the godless:
the endless pursuit of pleasure,
the ceaseless striving for satisfaction.
I seek only communion with You:
to be one with Christ,[8]
forged in the fire of Your love.[9]

The gifts of God
for the people of God[10]
are a cup overflowing,
an endless feast.

In highest regard
I hold You, Lord—
Master,
Redeemer,
Friend.

I esteem Your Way,
Your Truth,
Your Life
above all else.

Amen.

6. John 3:7. 7. 2 Cor. 5:17. 8. 1 Cor. 6:17. 9. 1 John 4:18. 10. Episcopal Church, *The Book of Common Prayer and Administration of the Sacraments and Other Rites and Ceremonies of the Church* (Oxford University Press, 1990), 364.

PROVERBS 14:29–30

IN MY ANGER

Like a cresting wave,
my anger
rises
and
descends,
crashing with merciless force
on all who oppose me.

In my anger,
keep me from sin, O Lord.[1]

When I look upon the wicked,
my soul seethes;
I burn with indignation at
iniquity,
injustice,
inhumanity.

History is a story of
wickedness run wild:
towers of Babel
and Babylon,
of promised peace,
Edenic splendor,
devolving into
chaos,
tyranny,
ruin.

1. Eph. 4:26–27.

The tumbled pillars of the past
are all that remain of every crooked kingdom
built in defiance of truth.

In my anger,
keep me from sin, O Lord.

My heart burns as I watch
history repeat itself:
as those made in the image of God are
seduced by every passion of the flesh,[2]
by the assurance of autonomy,
the relinquishment of constraint,
only to find themselves imprisoned
by the very things that promised freedom.

I fume with holy zeal.
Self-control escapes me.
Grace eludes me.
Left to my own devices,
I am as merciless as those who defy You.

God,
destroy the destroyers!
May devastation fall upon all
who seek to extinguish
the light of Your glory,
who trample upon truth,
who make a mockery of the good,
mar the beautiful.

I long for vengeance,
for a just punishment of the wicked—
but You alone are judge.

2. Rom. 7:5.

In my anger,
keep me from sin, O Lord.

Only by the power of Your Spirit[3]
can I resist
bitterness,
resentment,
hate
and embrace the way of
empathy,
gentleness,[4]
kindness.[5]

In the face of injustice,
may my mouth be an implement of truth,
seasoned with grace.

In the face of suffering,
may my hand be an implement of mercy,
anointed with compassion.

May I walk in perfect peace,
my mind stayed upon You.[6]

Teach me to
love with conviction,
dissent with grace,
behold Your image
even in the face of my enemies.

Lord Jesus,
Rabbi,
Master,

3. 1 Cor. 2:12. 4. Matt. 11:29; Eph. 4:2. 5. Col. 3:12. 6. Isa. 26:3.

the God in whom I trust—
in my anger,
keep me from sin.

Amen.

PROVERBS 15:1–2, 4, 7

A GENTLE ANSWER

In a world of careless words,
a gentle answer
is a difficult grace to give.

Lord,
may I be ready to answer,[1]
in season,
out of season,
by the power of Your Holy Spirit.

In a marketplace of idols,
harsh talk comes easily.
Fire fights fire;
rebuke meets rebuke.

Form in me a holy restraint,
for a gentle answer turns away wrath.[2]

May the words of my mouth
still violent waters,
heal violent hearts.

May I seek to embody
understanding,
compassion,
charity.

To speak truth to opposition,
to remain composed in confrontation—
this is Your way.

1. 1 Pet. 3:15–16. 2. Prov. 15:1.

To seek common ground without compromise,
to speak peace in the midst of violence—
this is Your way.

To dignify others while honoring You,
to offer wisdom rather than sentiment,
answers rather than abstractions—
this is Your way.

The Spirit-fruit of gentleness[3]
is a sign of Your presence—
carving a path through the wilderness[4]
where no path could otherwise be found.

May my lips be ready to answer
the unreasonable,
the unreachable,
the unteachable—
with the grace of God.[5]

For with You all things are possible.[6]

3. Gal. 5:22–23. 4. Isa. 43:19. 5. John 1:16. 6. Matt. 19:26.

PROVERBS 15:13, 16–17

SPIRIT OF GRATITUDE

Father,
cultivate in me
a spirit of gratitude today[1]—
that I may discern Your hand
in all my comings and goings,
the manifold work of Your Spirit
in all manner of things.

For benevolence,
provision,
contentment,
I thank You.[2]

For days of
joy,
hope,
delight,
I thank You.

For every provision,
every gift,
every blessing,
I thank You.[3]

For laughter
that lifts the heavy heart,
for the oil of gladness
that soothes the troubled spirit,
I thank You.

1. 1 Thess. 5:18. 2. Ps. 107:1. 3. James 1:17.

For the nearness of friends,
the listening ear,
the comforting touch,
I thank You.

To encounter Your glory
in everyday life,
to recognize Your sovereign work
moment by moment,
breath by breath,
is my prayer.

You are Lord
of things great and small:
galactic and granular,
cosmic and atomic,
indisputable and imperceptible.

It is good to give thanks to You,
to sing Your praises,
to declare Your unending love,
to proclaim Your enduring faithfulness.[4]

For countless mercies
too many to number,
I thank You.[5]

4. Ps. 92:1–2. 5. Lam. 3:22–23.

PROVERBS 15:22

THE COUNSEL OF THE GODLY

Surround me, Holy Spirit,
with the counsel of the godly,
that I may be
guided,
guarded,
grounded.

May I befriend those
who feast upon Your Word,
drink deeply of Your love,
who thrive in
righteousness,
holiness,
humility.

May my spirit be
submissive,
attentive,
teachable—
that I may discern
wisdom from folly,
truth from falsehood.

May I not be wise in my own eyes.[1]
May I fear You,
love You,

1. Prov. 26:12.

turn away from evil,
embrace
instruction,
correction,
direction.

Surround me with
compassionate hearts—
those who care for
the weak,
the vulnerable,
the poor.[2]

Surround me with those
committed to
justice,
kindness,
equity.

Surround me with
listening ears—
those who care greatly,
serve selflessly,
walk humbly.[3]

Surround me, O Lord,
with the counsel of the godly,
that I may be
guided,
guarded,
grounded.

Amen.

2. Prov. 29:7. 3. Mic. 6:8.

PROVERBS 16:1–3, 6–7, 9

THE PLAN OF THE LORD

The plan of the Lord
is faithful and true,[1]
an orchestration of grace over
moments,
hours,
days,
years—
for the flourishing of my soul,
the sanctification of my will,
the redemption of my future.

What is the measure of our days?
We race to outrun the hands of time,
but death comes for us all;
from dust we come,
to dust we return.[2]

I make my plans, Lord,
but You determine my steps.

We are cursed by transience.
We stumble down dead ends,
away from
life,
light,
liberty.

1. Ps. 33:4. 2. Gen. 3:19.

We labor in the light of the sun
until the dusk of death descends.
We diminish,
dissipate,
disappear
into the quiet of the grave.

I make my plans, Lord,
but You determine my steps.

Though we waste away,
we who have the mind of Christ[3]
are inwardly renewed,[4]
going from glory to glory.[5]

True life is following You,
keeping step with the Spirit,[6]
trusting in Your goodness,
learning to
value what You value,
prize what You prize,
seek what You seek.[7]

We see in part.
We know in part.[8]

So often I lose my way,
stumbling in darkness
with no compass or guide,
beholden to
change,
opinion,
opportunity,
accident.

3. 1 Cor. 2:16. 4. 2 Cor. 4:16. 5. 2 Cor. 3:18. 6. Gal. 5:25. 7. Matt. 6:33.
8. 1 Cor. 13:12.

So often I expect You to honor my
wants,
needs,
intentions
within the limits of measurable time,
according to the limits of my patience.

And yet,
You weigh my heart.[9]

The wasted hours
You redeem.
The lost years
You reclaim.

Through discipline
You conform me
to the image of Christ.[10]

I make my plans, Lord,
but You determine my steps.

Teach me, Lord,
to number my days,[11]
to walk with eternity in mind,[12]
to keep time by the measure of Your grace,
to greet every moment as a gift from Your hands.

Then peace will be my portion,
joy my companion,
endurance my strength.

The plan of the Lord
is faithful and true,

9. Prov. 21:2. 10. Rom. 8:29. 11. Ps. 39:4. 12. Eccles. 3:11.

an orchestration of grace over
moments,
hours,
days,
years—
for the flourishing of my soul,
the sanctification of my will,
the redemption of my future.

Direct my steps, Lord.

Amen.

PROVERBS 16:25

PRIDE'S CUP

Lord,
I have lifted pride's cup
to the heavens,
elevated my achievements,
deified my dreams;
I have reveled in adoration,
in victory;
wallowed in despair,
in defeat;
perceived myself to be
immune,
immovable,
impenetrable.

How clear is my vision
when it concerns me!
How quick is my step
when my reputation is at risk!

In my self-absorption,
my ever-expanding efforts to influence,
I have celebrated my own accomplishments
rather than the patient work of God in me.

Woe is me.

I have betrayed You
in matters large and small;
invested time and energy
into work

born of my own selfish ambition
rather than Your will.[1]

I have pardoned myself for
partial obedience,
half trust,
fickle faith.
I have turned a blind eye to
my own weakness,
waywardness,[2]
wantonness.

The heart is deceitful;
who can know it?[3]

Like all my fallen brothers and sisters,
I excel at self-deception;
I fall prey to idolatry;
I retain a form of godliness
while denying its power.[4]

Who will save me from this body of death?[5]

Lord of my desires,
may I wake each day with
renewed passion for Your ways,
godly discernment of Your will,
wisely stewarding the time You have
given,
bestowed,
gifted—
rather than squandering it.

1. Heb. 10:7–9. 2. Rom. 3:23. 3. Jer. 17:9. 4. 2 Tim. 3:2–5. 5. Rom. 7:24.

I have seen You in the sanctuary,
beheld Your power and glory;[6]
I bow down in worship—
release all attachments,
surrender all fears,[7]
anchor my spirit in Your Spirit,
that I may be strengthened to
resist temptation,
sidestep ruin,
walk in the light of life.

I commit to Your way,[8]
led by Your hand,
guided in quietness
and confidence
and strength.[9]

Teach me to walk through life
with reverent fear,
to resist the spell of lesser loves.

Grant me eyes to see[10]
the poor,
the needy,
the vulnerable;
widen my heart
to meet the needs around me;
to extend grace,
generosity,
understanding.

My eyes are dim, Lord;
I peer through a glass darkly.[11]
Increase my vision to see
as You see,

6. Ps. 63:2. 7. 1 John 4:18. 8. Matt. 7:13–14. 9. Isa. 30:15. 10. Luke 10:23. 11. 1 Cor. 13:12.

that my plans may align—
day in,
day out—
with Your perfect will.[12]

Amen.

12. Rom. 12:2.

PROVERBS 16:31

PASS THE YEARS

Moment by moment,
day by day,
age pursues me.

My body slows,
my mind blurs,
as I inch closer to the grave.

Lord,
may I pass the years
in union with You.[1]

My body,
Your temple,[2]
I will care for as
a gardener tends soil.
May good and healthy fruit
blossom from these branches—
fruits of
strength,
capacity,
resilience,
for Your kingdom.

Lord,
may I pass the years
in union with You.

1. John 17:20–23. 2. 1 Cor. 6:19.

With age,
may I win wisdom.
With length of days,
may I attain understanding.[3]

Even as this outer self wastes away,
as these leaves turn autumn gold,
You are renewing me.[4]

A weight of glory[5]
awaits the heart that grows in grace.

Lord,
may I pass the years
in union with You.

Renew me, Lord,
day by day,
as I look beyond the seen
to the unseen,
my eyes fixed upon You:[6]
my unbroken hope,
my love and longing,
my joy eternal.

See if there be
any wicked way in me.
Lead me in
everlasting,[7]
unending
fullness
of life;
health of
heart,

3. Job 12:12. 4. Isa. 40:31. 5. 2 Cor. 4:17. 6. Heb. 12:2. 7. Ps. 139:24.

body,
mind,
soul—
that I may know You,
worship You,
and enjoy You forever.[8]

Amen.

8. Inspired by the Westminster Catechism.

PROVERBS 17:1

IN SILENCE

In silence,
solitude,
stillness,
I find rest.[1]

My soul is quieted within me.[2]
I sit at the feet of the Covenant God,
stare into the eyes of a loving Father,
release my cares to Your kindness.

I wait patiently for You[3]—
for You are good to those who hope in You,
to the one who seeks You with a whole heart.[4]

In silence,
solitude,
stillness,
I find rest.

I am trained in the holy space of silence,
to listen rather than speak,
to tune my heart to the frequency of Your Spirit.

When I meditate upon You,
when all my attention is focused on Your presence,
You fill me with a peace surpassing understanding,[5]
guarding my heart and mind
in Christ Jesus.[6]

1. Matt. 11:29. 2. Ps. 131:2. 3. Ps. 37:7. 4. Lam. 3:25–26. 5. Isa. 26:3. 6. Phil. 4:7.

In silence,
solitude,
stillness,
I find rest.

I condition my soul
to embrace solitude
in the midst of chaos,
to take captive every thought[7]
with the mind of Christ.[8]

My soul finds rest in You,
my Rock,
my Salvation,
my Fortress.[9]

In silence,
solitude,
stillness,
I find rest.

I host stillness in my body,
slowing to the rhythm of Your shalom,
restlessness giving way to repose.

You are Lord of the Sabbath,[10]
gentle and humble of heart,[11]
calling all who are
weary,
burdened,
anxious,
fearful
to take Your yoke upon them—
for Your yoke is easy

7. 2 Cor. 10:5. 8. 1 Cor. 2:16. 9. Ps. 62:1–2. 10. Matt. 12:8. 11. Matt. 11:29.

and Your burden is light,
and in You our souls find rest.[12]

In silence,
solitude,
stillness,
I find rest.

May silence become song,
solitude become sanctuary,
stillness become freedom,
all for Your glory.

Amen.

12. Matt. 11:28–30.

PROVERBS 17:3

MATURE AND COMPLETE

A vision of glory awaits me
on the far side of suffering—
my faith proved genuine,
perseverance finishing its perfect work.[1]

I have known hope deferred,[2]
dreams shattered,
only to be reborn
and reformed
by Your Spirit
into a more beautiful destiny
than I could have imagined.

In Your good timing,
momentary struggle
yields the peaceful fruit of righteousness.[3]

Lord,
forgive my stumbling.
Purify the thoughts and intentions
of my heart.

Each day brings new trials,
exposing my fragility,
my vulnerability,
my obstinacy.

Search me and know me.
Test my inmost thoughts.

1. James 1:4. 2. Prov. 13:12. 3. Heb. 12:11.

See if there be any wicked way in me.
Lead me in everlasting ways.[4]

A quiet arrogance persists
behind this veil of humility;
I still insist upon my own way,
in an effort to maintain a posture of control.

Who has known Your mind that we would teach You?[5]
Who has imagined what You have imagined into being?[6]

I seek maturity in faith,
fullness of purpose,
growth in grace,
as I look to You:
keeper of my heart.

I resist evil,
embrace good.[7]

May I become
slow to anger,
quick to love,[8]
a friend of sinners,[9]
a guide to wanderers,
a help to the helpless,
a light in darkness,
a voice of reason,
a contented child of God—
bring me to wholeness
as I learn the way of service;
may my actions prove
wisdom's good work in me.[10]

4. Ps. 139:24. 5. Rom. 11:34. 6. Job 38:4–41. 7. Rom. 12:9–10. 8. Ps. 103:8. 9. Matt. 11:19. 10. Matt. 11:19.

You took on the nature of a servant,
clothed in human likeness.[11]
In humility,
You modeled selfless love.[12]

Help me, Lord,
to submit to Your Spirit,
that I may be trained in righteousness:
purified,[13]
mature,
complete,
not lacking in any good thing.[14]

Amen.

11. Phil 2:5–8. 12. Phil. 2:3. 13. Matt. 5:8. 14. James 1:4.

PROVERBS 17:9, 17

THE WISDOM OF FRIENDSHIP

I will be
my brother's keeper,
my sister's guardian,
caregiver of my companions,
champion of my family.

When I fail a friend, Lord,
forgive me.[1]
When a friend fails me,
grant me the strength to forgive[2]—
to cover them with the same grace
that covers me.[3]

By this everyone will know that you are my disciples,
if you love one another.[4]

There is no end to gossip,
words that pierce the heart[5]
and wound the spirit.
May such talk be far from me,
my voice speaking encouragement
rather than discouragement.

Let us love one another,
for love is from God,
and whoever loves has been born of God.[6]

1. Mic. 7:18. 2. Matt. 6:12. 3. John 1:16. 4. John 13:35. 5. Prov. 16:28; Eph. 4:29. 6. 1 John 4:7.

May I take every opportunity to
extend mercy,
embody love,[7]
exhibit kindness.

May I receive as openly as I give,
for I, too, am in need of affection.

Clothe yourselves with
compassion,
kindness,
humility,
gentleness,
patience.[8]

In suffering,
may I remember that friendship is forged in trial,
that there is no greater love
than to lay down one's life for another.[9]

Be in debt to no one;
save for your debt to each other—
for he who loves others has fulfilled the law.[10]

When the redeemed of the Lord dwell in unity,
it is a holy anointing,
a christening with the oil of gladness[11]—
for the world will know we are Your beloved
by our love for one another.[12]

Amen.

7. 1 Cor. 12:31–13:13. 8. Col. 3:12. 9. John 15:13. 10. Rom. 13:8.
11. Ps. 133:1–2. 12. John 13:35.

PROVERBS 17:22

ORCHARD OF JOY

Row upon row,
vine upon vine
grows the Orchard of Joy
in the fields of God.

The harvest of the Spirit
hangs heavy upon the branches,
ripe and sweet,
each stem nurtured and tended
by the Great Orchardist,
life springing forth in exuberant increase,
new wine flowing from the hills.[1]

Gardener of Grace,[2]
I walk with You
through the Orchard of Joy
in the cool of the evening,
my soul released from fear,
my heart lifted from sadness,
my mind delivered from despair.

"Come," You call;
"Come, beloved one!
The frosts of winter have passed,
the winds and rain have abated,
leaving the bounty of spring—
a flowering feast."[3]

1. Amos 9:13. 2. John 15:1. 3. Song of Sol. 2:11–12.

By Your provision,
the barren wasteland is made glad,
the desert rejoices in song,
the arid ground blossoms like the crocus.[4]

When I am parched,
barren,
fruitless,
dust and bones in the cool earth,
resurrect me;
raise me to newness of life.[5]

May I feed upon Truth,
drink deeply of Love,
abide in intimate communion—
for I can do nothing apart from You.[6]

Amen.

4. Isa. 35:1. 5. Rom. 6:4. 6. John 15:5.

PROVERBS 18:10–12

A HUMBLE LIFE

Lord,
I place my trust in You
again today—
not in
temporary gain,[1]
momentary vigor,
fleeting plans.[2]

You have been my help
in times of need,[3]
my strength
when all else failed me.[4]

I part ways with those who
preach the empty promises of this world.
I resist all voices proclaiming peace
in anything apart from You.

To know You
and the power of Your resurrection,[5]
to walk in fullness of life,
is my deepest desire.

I will run to You
when the battle rages,
when the ranks of my oppressors
swell like waves of the sea—
for the righteous find safety in Your arms.

1. Matt. 6:19–20. 2. Prov. 16:9. 3. Ps. 27:9. 4. Heb. 13:5–6. 5. Phil. 3:10–11.

In You
this roving spirit finds rest.[6]
You are the strength of my heart
and my portion forever.[7]

Some trust in chariots,
some in princes,
but I trust in Your name,
O Lord.[8]

In this house I will proclaim,
"The name of the Lord is a mighty respite;
there is no safety apart from Him."

The godless take comfort
in the illusion of security—
in transient refuges of
fortune and fame—
until disaster falls.

In calamity,
they run from You—
hiding behind boastful speech,
ignoring their own soul-sickness.

With every step away from grace,
their spirits diminish all the more,
until they are but a pale shadow of Your handiwork.

The pride of life—
lusts and longings pursued,[9]
the vain imagination that accompanies arrogance[10]—
is their undoing;
they are devoured by the gods they worship.

6. Matt. 11:28. 7. Ps. 73:26. 8. Ps. 20:7. 9. 1 John 2:16. 10. Rom. 1:21.

When strength diminishes,
the pillars of their empires crumble;
when death comes,
the ruin of their lives is laid bare.

Honor is found not in
ephemeral beauty,
worldly success,
the relentless quest for satisfaction,
but in the humble life[11]
of one who
trusts,
hopes,
places confidence
in the name of the Lord.

Lord,
I place my trust in You today.

Amen.

11. Matt. 11:29.

PROVERBS 18:21

CARE FOR MY WORDS

I will care for my words, Lord,
for they wield the power of life and death.[1]

Intentional with my tongue,
merciful with my mouth,
I will bless,
encourage,
empower.

Words written,
spoken,
whispered,
shouted
have the power to
wound,
heal,
build up,
tear down.

A tender heart
scarred by careless speech
is slow to recover.

An innocent soul
stung by rebuke
carries its grief into full age.

But, Lord, when did we see You
hungry and in need?[2]

1. Prov. 18:21. 2. Matt. 25:31–46.

When I have seen others
starved for kindness,
in need of a gentle word,
have I spoken in love,
or am I nothing more than a noisy gong
or a clanging cymbal?[3]

Blessed are those
who know the power of the tongue
and master it.[4]

May my mouth be an agent of truth,
overflowing with Your grace—
that those I meet today may
see,
hear,
feel
Your affection
through me.

May all who see me
see Christ;
may all who hear me
hear Christ.[5]
May all I touch
be touched by Your love.

Lord,
I will care for my words,
for in them You have placed the power
of life and death.

3. 1 Cor. 13:1. 4. James 3:1–11. 5. This line resonates with "St. Patrick's Breastplate" (*Lorica*) of the Irish prayer tradition.

PROVERBS 18:24

YOU CALL ME FRIEND

Father God,
You call me friend.[1]

My life,
for all its twists and turns,
its sorrows and desolations,
is the story of one loved by the God
who calls me friend.

When I stagger in the deepest dark,
when I flee to the ends of the earth,
You follow me.[2]

Your correction is a comfort.[3]
Your mercy is a meal set before me.
Never do You leave me.
Never do You forsake me.[4]

You call me friend.

Where can I hide[5]
from One who is closer than a brother,[6]
who saves me from endless wandering,
invites me into the fellowship of the saints?

Impart Your truth to me, O God,
that I may carry Your glory
in this mortal frame,
a temple for the indwelling of Your Spirit.[7]

1. John 15:15. 2. Ps. 139:7–12. 3. Prov. 3:12. 4. Heb. 13:5. 5. Ps. 139:7. 6. Prov. 18:24. 7. 1 Cor. 6:19.

When righteousness thrives
and hearts are made whole,
meet me in my joy.

When grief descends
and pain threatens,
meet me in my suffering.[8]

In every circumstance,
I entrust myself to my faithful Creator,
co-laboring with You
to sow seeds of resurrection life
in the land of my sojourn.

No name or accolade,
prize or praise
means more to me
than the knowledge of this truth:

You call me friend.

When hope is out of reach,
when faith is a half-forgotten dream,
You will not forsake me;
You will lift my heart from trouble.[9]

Father God,
You call me friend.

8. 1 Pet. 4:19. 9. John 14:1.

PROVERBS 19:17

THE LORD PROVIDES

To be generous
is to be wise;
to be wise
is to be generous.

To be generous
is to be like You, God;
to be like You, God,
is to be generous.

Storehouses of heaven open
when my hands are open,
when I allow Your grace to flow in me
and through me
to those in need.

The Lord provides.[1]

You have blessed me
with extravagant provision,
Your mercies overflowing—
while there are those who face
hunger,
loss,
lack.

Teach me to walk in generosity,[2]
to turn to others with a ready heart
and a ready hand,

1. Gen. 22:14. 2. 1 Tim. 6:18.

eagerly seeking how I might
bless the needy,
console the suffering,
aid the destitute.

Where can I give, Lord?
With whom can I share?

Those paralyzed by fear.
Weakened by scarcity.
Oppressed by sin.

If You have set my feet upon a rock,
made my footsteps firm,[3]
grant me the strength to reach beyond comfort,
to lift others to safety.

For those who would save their life will lose it,
but those who lose their life for You will find it.[4]

To be generous
is to be wise;
to be wise
is to be generous.

To be generous
is to be like You, God;
to be like You, God,
is to be generous.

Storehouses of heaven open
when my hands are open,
when I allow Your grace to flow in me

3. Ps. 40:2. 4. Matt. 16:25.

and through me
to those in need.

The Lord provides.

PROVERBS 19:21, 23

DIRECT MY STEPS

Lord,
how often have I,
from restlessness
or arrogance,
acted without Your blessing?
Moved without Your leading?

Starved for vision,
impatient in waiting,
I have formulated plans,
determined steps
toward the life I desired,
confident in my own self-sufficiency.

Those who wait upon the Lord
shall renew their strength.[1]

Left to my own devices,
I am a slave to
safety,
security,
freedom
from want
or suffering.

A soul makes plans,
but the Lord directs the steps.[2]

1. Isa. 40:31. 2. Prov. 16:9.

Often I miss the quiet way:
the slow surrender of desire,
the patient attention of prayer.

Help me, Lord,
to wait upon You,
to listen for
confirmation,
correction,
counsel.
Teach me to keep step with the Spirit,[3]
to discern the mystery of Your will—
that which is
good,
acceptable,
perfect.[4]

May I look beyond present circumstances,
measuring all things
in light of eternity.

Direct my steps today, Lord.

3. Gal. 5:25. 4. Rom. 12:2.

PROVERBS 20:22

FREE INDEED

Lord,
there is pain in this world
beyond comprehension.
At every turn,
echoes of the Fall—
the death of
trust,
innocence,
faith—
surround me.

Grace and forgiveness escape us
as we war through the wilderness,
as soul meets soul on the battleground:
a relentless violence,
a never-ending struggle.

Every square inch of this
war-torn earth is scarred by
oppression,
subjugation,
wickedness,
ruin.

It is our sin-bent nature:
a generational curse,
an illness of the heart.

Peer into my heart, O Lord,
reveal my motives with Your Word;[1]

1. Heb. 4:12.

give me eyes to recognize my own weakness,
the sin lurking in my own soul.[2]
Remind me that vengeance is Yours,
that in Your good timing
justice will be done;
all will be made well.

Lord Jesus,
You embodied a better way—
the path of
life,
wholeness,
beauty—
the cruciform way of mercy.

We know not what we do.[3]

As wickedness increases,
may we wait with hopeful expectation.
As sin seeps into every good and beautiful thing,
may we remember that
we are on earth,
You are in heaven,
and that our words should be few.[4]

Creation groans,
longing for the revealing of the sons of God.[5]

Lord,
where I am sin-bent
from within and without,
let peace prevail in my soul;
let repentance do its work.
When I am afflicted by others,
scorned without cause,

2. Rom. 7:21–25. 3. Luke 23:34. 4. Eccles. 5:2. 5. Rom. 8:19.

may I be slow to speak,
slow to anger.[6]

Where I am tempted to
hate,
reject,
despise,
may I be born anew to
love,
bless,
entrust to You
every enemy of my soul—
that Your will,
not my own,
would be done.[7]

"Vengeance is mine,"
says the Lord.[8]

Come quickly, Lord Jesus.[9]
Right every wrong.
Mend all that is broken.
Execute justice in the earth.

Look upon me, Lord;
answer the cry of my heart.
May I judge not,
that I may not be judged;
may I walk humbly in the way of grace,
that I may be free indeed.[10]

Amen.

6. James 1:19. 7. Matt. 6:10. 8. Rom. 12:19. 9. Rev. 22:20. 10. John 8:36.

PROVERBS 20:23

WHO IS MY NEIGHBOR?

Father God,
break my heart
for the mistreatment of the lowly,[1]
the oppression of the destitute.

Disciple me in
the tending of bruised reeds,[2]
the preaching of good news to the poor,
the liberation of the captives[3]—
that the voiceless
may be given voice.

Who is my neighbor, Lord?[4]

Counsel me in the ways of
restoring and uplifting
the neglected and dismissed,
the frail and forgotten,
the family-less and friendless,
the huddled and desperate,
the widow and orphan,
the poor and marginalized,
the wandering and wanting.

May I be bold to stand against
the ways of the wicked,
who seek gain from another's misfortune.[5]

1. Prov. 31:8–9; Jer. 22:3. 2. Isa. 42:3; Matt. 12:20. 3. Luke 4:18–19.
4. Luke 10:25–37. 5. Ps. 146:7–9.

May I not be silent
when guilt adorns
the wayward,
when they drift down paths of destruction.

May the wise be awakened
to the plight of the vulnerable,
that they may care in prayer and action,
interceding for the weak
until the Sun of Righteousness
rises with healing in His wings.[6]

May I hear,
obey,
receive Your Word,
humble myself in repentance—
aware of my own culpability,
my tendency to use others
for my own interest,
to use false scales
weighed in my favor.

May I not judge in another
what I refuse to recognize in myself.[7]

May I not withhold good
from the one who deserves it,[8]
nor refuse to extend mercy
to the one in need of it.

May I extend my hand
to the fallen,
extend Your kindness
to all within my reach.

6. Mal. 4:2. 7. Matt. 7:1–5. 8. Prov. 3:27.

May I resist my selfish desire for gain,
seeking instead the welfare of others,
that I may lift the weak,
encourage the downcast,
heal the broken,
in Your name.

May I embody Your loving-kindness,
ushering my neighbors
into the presence of the Living God,
into true freedom,
joyful absolution,
eternal rest.

Amen.

PROVERBS 21:1–3

I SEEK YOUR FAVOR

Lord,
who has known Your mind?[1]
Who has understood Your ways?
The orchestration of Your glory
in the lives of humankind?

The powers of this world
believe themselves to be
untouchable,
impenetrable,
unaccountable—
but You are the One who turns
darkness to light,[2]
chaos to order,
the One who guides the heart,
sways the will,
directs the mind
to accomplish Your
great and glorious purposes.

You are righteous in all Your ways,
kind in all Your works.[3]

When I digress,
seeking my own way,
Your hand directs me;
Your voice assures me:
"This is the way;
walk in it."[4]

1. Rom. 11:34. 2. John 8:12. 3. Ps. 145:17. 4. Isa. 30:21.

By Your grace and intervention
I am rescued from ruin,
set upon the path of life.

To obey is better than sacrifice.[5]
To act justly,
love mercy,
walk humbly with You
is what You require.[6]

When I am too comfortable
to recognize the needs around me,
when I am blind to
poverty,
shame,
loss—
You strike me with
holy discontent.
You stir my heart
to compassionate response.

Those who love You
obey You;[7]
those who seek You
find You.[8]
Your presence sustains them
all the days of their lives.

O Lord,
I seek Your favor,
and Yours alone today.

Amen.

5. 1 Sam. 15:22. 6. Mic. 6:8. 7. John 14:15. 8. Jer. 29:13.

PROVERBS 21:21

LORD OF MERCY

Lord of Mercy,
the grace You bestow on me
is too marvelous,
too wondrous
to comprehend.[1]

To walk in intimacy with You—
companioned by Your gentleness,
lovingly disciplined in the Way of Life—
is my heart's desire.[2]

I am far too easily driven to
anger,[3]
arrogance,
bitterness,
impatience
than restrained by
kindness,
humility,
grace,
forbearance.

Forgive me, Lord.

Lord of Mercy,
who have I in heaven but You?
Who on earth do I desire but You?[4]

1. Ps. 131:1. 2. Ps. 27:4. 3. Exod. 34:6. 4. Ps. 73:25.

Today I will have
opportunity to turn toward
my brother,
my sister,
my neighbor,
my enemy
with gentleness or harshness,
compassion or disregard,
openness or contempt.

By Your strength,
may I embody the way of Jesus,
gentle and humble in heart,[5]
who, though He was equal with God the Father,
emptied Himself as a servant.[6]

Lord of Mercy,
hear me;
attend to my prayer.[7]

5. Matt. 11:29. 6. Phil. 2:1–11. 7. Ps. 102:1–2.

PROVERBS 21:30-31

I WILL NOT BE SHAKEN

O my soul,
I will begin today in victory—
the victory of the Lord my God.[1]

At the first blush of dawn,
I will meditate on His promises,[2]
faithfully kept by
the God of Covenant,[3]
who showers me with blessings.

Greater is He who is in me
than the one who is in the world.[4]

I will not be shaken.
I will not be moved.[5]

At the rising of the sun,
I will breathe in the peace of His presence,
secure in His love.

Conflict awaits me—
a chorus of untruth in my ears,
a host of graven images
vying for my affection.

I will not be shaken.
I will not be moved.

Before the day is done,
I will see truth vanquish lies,

1. 1 Cor. 15:57. 2. Ps. 119:27. 3. Neh. 1:5. 4. 1 John 4:4. 5. Ps. 16:8.

mercy triumph over judgment[6]—
for I have kept His Word in my
heart,
soul,
mind,[7]
that I may remember
who I am,
who He is,
the hope He has called me to,
the riches
of His glorious inheritance
in the saints.[8]

I will not be shaken.
I will not be moved.

Do not be downcast,
O my soul;
your hope is in God[9]—
the God whose victory is secure over all
death and darkness,
sin and sorrow,
pain and sickness.

I will begin today in victory—
the victory of the Lord my God—
for His mercies are new every morning.[10]

Amen.

6. James 2:13. 7. Ps. 119:11. 8. Eph. 1:18. 9. Ps. 42:5. 10. Lam. 3:22–23.

PROVERBS 22:1–2, 4

A GOOD NAME

Lord,
what is the value of a name?

In the thirst for glory,
kings are unseated,
war is waged,
civilizations rise and fall.

In pursuit of honor,
blood is shed,
friendship scorned,
integrity abandoned.

You have called me by name;
I am Yours.[1]

In a world of
shame,
indignity,
accusation,[2]
care of one's position
is a daily toil.

Reputation,
like beauty,
is fleeting—
but the one who fears the Lord
remains forever,[3]

1. Isa. 43:1. 2. Matt. 5:11–12. 3. Prov. 9:10.

generation
to generation.

You have called me by name;
I am Yours.

Measures of worldly significance
will pass away
in the presence of
the Naming God,
who calls us His own.

The name You declare over me—
one of
belovedness,
adoption,
adoration—
is all I seek.

In humility I bow before You,
Maker of Heaven and Earth,
who calls me by name—
the name engraved upon the palms of Your hands,[4]
inscribed upon a white stone,[5]
written in Your book of life,[6]
spoken over me from before I was born.[7]

I am the beloved of God.

You have called me by name;
I am Yours.

4. Isa. 49:16. 5. Rev. 2:17. 6. Rev. 3:5. 7. Jer. 1:5.

PROVERBS 22:6

PRAYER FOR THE WAYWARD

Father,
it is a long and winding way
on which You
teach us,
train us,
instruct us,
guide us
toward wholeness
and the prospering
of our souls.

Yet we fall,
wander,
disappoint ourselves
and one another.

All the while
You shepherd us,
tend to us,
with gentle leading
and a correcting hand.[1]

Have mercy on the prodigals
who run from Your presence,
who seek solace in all the wrong places,
for not all who wander are lost.[2]

1. John 10:27. 2. From J. R. R. Tolkien, *The Fellowship of the Ring* (Ballantine Books, 1965), 213.

Shepherd of Our Souls,
pursue the wayward,
heal the broken spirit,
forgive the penitent heart,
redeem the years the locust has eaten.[3]

May I be like You:
Pursuer of the Lost,
Lover of the Sojourner.

May I take my place as
intercessor,
leader,
friend,
raising and nurturing others
to full maturity.

May I not let go
of the hem of Your garment
until You bless them,[4]
deliver them,
set them on the path to life.[5]

In Your presence there is joy and gladness.

I will ponder the mysteries of God
in the quiet of my heart,[6]
that I may be equipped for every good work.[7]

You do not demand our trust,
force our obedience,
compel our surrender.

Lord,
give me patience
to bear with the struggles of the weak.

3. Joel 2:25. 4. Matt. 9:20–22. 5. Ps. 16:11. 6. Luke 2:19. 7. 2 Tim. 3:16–17.

You stand at the door and knock[8]—
patient,
long-suffering,
storing up mercy for the penitent heart.

May I not be a hindrance or a stumbling block
for those who are slow to surrender.

In good time,
may all who scorn You
praise You.
May all who run from You
run to You.
May all who wander from You
return to You—
that they may be healed[9]
and find life everlasting.

Amen.

8. Rev. 3:20. 9. Isa. 6:10.

PROVERBS 22:22–23

REMEMBER THE POOR

Lord,
there was but one thing
the apostle Paul was eager to do
when sent out from Jerusalem—
he longed to remember the poor.[1]

May I follow his example.

To those who are
hungry,
thirsty,
weak,
discarded,
misguided,
misunderstood,
ill,
afraid,
lost—
here am I, Lord;
send me.[2]

To those who are
weary,
desperate,
frail,
forgotten,
deluded,
deceived,

1. Gal. 2:10. 2. Isa. 6:8.

faint,
doubtful,
ruined—
here am I, Lord;
send me.

Is it not Your desire to
lift the poor from the dust?
Seat them with princes in places of honor?[3]

You take up the cause of the needy;
show me how to plead their case before others.

You attend to the troubled of mind;
show me how to bind up hidden wounds.[4]

You give grace to the poor and impoverished;
show me how to share with open hands.

You companion souls who live in desperation;
show me how to care with an understanding heart.

You see the rejected and abandoned;
show me how to seek and find the lost.

You visit the lonely in spirit;
show me how to extend the mercy of friendship.[5]

You grant inward strength to the fallen;
show me how to raise others from the mire.

You embrace the isolated and disheartened;
show me how to walk in true compassion.

You reach out to the wounded and discarded;
show me how to minister with kindness.

3. 1 Sam. 2:8. 4. Ps. 147:3. 5. Ps. 68:6.

You keep the weary from stumbling;
show me how to be a listening ear.

You lighten the load of the wanderer;
show me how to be a voice of
refreshment,[6]
renewal,
reconciliation.[7]

If I close my heart to those in need,
how does Your love abide in me?[8]

Help me, O God,
to be rich in good works[9]—
for whatever I do unto the least of these,
I do unto You.[10]

6. Mark 9:41. 7. 2 Cor. 5:18. 8. 1 John 3:17. 9. 1 Tim. 6:18. 10. Matt. 25:40.

PROVERBS 22:29

BLESS THE WORKER

Lord,
bless the worker,
who labors with
body,
mind,
spirit,
skill—
that endeavors may be accomplished,
duty and diligence revealed.

Lord,
bless the worker,
who labors for
provision,
sustenance,
influence,
vision—
that beauty would be manifested,
acts of care and service fulfilled.

Lord,
bless the worker,
who labors with
diligence,
courage,
character,
will—

that calling and delight would be one,
feats of soul and spirit sustained.

May we work with fullness of heart,
as for You
and not for human accolades,[1]
pursuing excellence in all
the work of our hands,
filled with Your Spirit of
wisdom,
understanding,
knowledge;
anointed with
ability,
capacity,
virtuosity[2]—
for the prospering of the earth,
the advancement of Your kingdom,
the proclamation of Your glory.

Lord,
bless the worker—
that we might stand with dignity
at the end of a hard day's labor,
thankful for the privilege of
ruling and reigning
over some small corner of creation,
imaging the Creator God,
whose favor goes before us.

Amen.

1. Col. 3:23. 2. Exod. 31:3.

PROVERBS 23:15–18

GOD OF MY FUTURE

God of my future,
lead me in the Way of Life.

You delight in my obedience,
revel in my worship.
Your heart rises
when my mouth speaks truth.
Your Spirit stirs heaven and earth
as I act with compassion
toward the suffering.

But I am a temperamental saint,
a half-hearted disciple.

Time and again
I aim for
truth,
nobility,
rightness,
purity—
only to be deceived,
dishonored,
debased,
degraded.

My sin is ever before me.[1]

Everywhere I look,
I see the wicked prospering—

1. Ps. 51:3.

unburdened by conscience,
unencumbered by the demands of righteousness.[2]

In my weakness,
I question Your faithfulness.
In my sin,
I question Your goodness.

I am a soul caught in liminal space,
suspended between conflicting desires,
a mystery to myself.

Remind me, Lord,
that You have the words of life,[3]
that in You is fullness of joy;
at Your right hand are pleasures forevermore.[4]

Remind me, Lord,
that You have called me to union with You[5]—
a future of unending delight,
unbroken peace.

This hour
I turn from envy,
from longings that war within my soul.
I embrace the fear of the Lord.
I begin anew.

Reinforce my hope.
Reignite my faith.
Reinvigorate my love,
that I may faithfully abide in You.[6]

Then I will be wise in Your eyes
rather than in my own;[7]

2. Ps. 73:1–12. 3. John 6:68. 4. Ps. 16:11. 5. John 15:4–5. 6. John 15:4–5. 7. Prov. 26:12.

I will wake each day to new mercies,[8]
lie down at night
in the safety of Your presence.[9]

Amen.

8. Lam. 3:22–23. 9. Ps. 31:20.

PROVERBS 23:29–35

LORD OF ALL BLESSINGS

Lord of All Blessings,
I am too easily satisfied.

Strung between
constraint and indulgence,
discipline and excess,
I am often guilty of treating good things
as ultimate things,
of clinging to Your gifts
rather than to You, the Giver.

When I am disoriented,
guide me back to truth;
help me to recognize my weakness,
lean upon Your strength,
walk in health of
mind,
body,
spirit.

May all that I do
be done in Your name.
Whether eating or drinking,
mourning or feasting—
I will revel in Your sovereignty,
in every good and perfect gift.[1]

May I resist the temptation of decadence:
of abusing Your provision

1. James 1:17.

so that appetite becomes compulsion,
enjoyment becomes dependency.

Lord of All Blessings,
fill me with delight,
ground me with gratitude,
guard me with discernment—
that I may walk in joy unspeakable[2]
and life eternal.[3]

Amen.

2. 1 Pet. 1:8. 3. John 10:10.

PROVERBS 24:3–6

THE COMMUNION OF THE SAINTS

Lord,
I am painfully aware of my limitations—
the insufficiency of my
wisdom,
knowledge,
understanding.[1]

I often feel as if I am living
in a half-built house
of fractured walls
and shattered ceilings,
open to the wind
and rain
and yawning dark.

In isolation,
I wither—
but in the communion of the saints,[2]
I am given
insight,
clarity,
a vision beyond my own.

When hope seems lost,
the counsel of a friend
is a light in the darkness.

1. Prov. 3:5. 2. Inspired by the Apostles' Creed.

For You have called us
to carry each other's burdens,[3]
to love one another
as You have loved us.[4]

I repent of my
selfishness,
self-dependence,
self-centeredness.

You have created me for community—
to flourish in friendship
and faithfulness.

Restore to us the vision of the Body of Christ:

Resplendent with beauty,
Your beloved will walk
in all the fullness of God.[5]

Vibrant with holiness,
Your beloved will flourish
in the midst of a crooked generation.[6]

Resounding with praise,
Your beloved will embody
the joy of Your presence.

Quickened by hope,
Your beloved will walk
in the power of Your promises.

Fashioned by fire,
Your beloved will mature
to the whole measure of the fullness of Christ.[7]

3. Gal. 6:2. 4. John 13:34. 5. Eph. 3:14–19. 6. Phil. 2:14–16. 7. Eph. 4:13.

Confronted by darkness,
Your beloved will shine
as a city set upon a hill.[8]

Perfected by suffering,
Your beloved will rise
in renewed strength.

Stirred by compassion,
Your beloved will declare
the wonders of Your mercy.

Carried by grace,
Your beloved will proclaim
the riches of Your pardon.

Compelled by love,
Your beloved will heal
the wounds of division and hate.[9]

Sanctified by Your Spirit,
Your beloved will carry
the aroma of Christ.[10]

By Your grace,
I am no longer a stranger,
an alien—
but a fellow citizen
with the saints,
a member of the
household of God.[11]

Amen.

8. Matt. 5:14. 9. Matt. 5:9. 10. 2 Cor. 2:15. 11. Eph. 2:19.

PROVERBS 24:11–12

RESCUE THE INNOCENT

Father,
forgive me for what I have done
and left undone.[1]

I have seen the plight of the innocent—
endless suffering,
unimaginable pain,
unfathomable sorrow—
without extending my hand in mercy.

The weight of this world
weighs heavy upon my heart.
I am paralyzed by
fear,
apathy,
indifference.

Show me, Lord,
how to be
merciful,
courageous,
selfless.

May Your kingdom come
on sin-sick earth
as in high and holy heaven.[2]

1. Episcopal Church, *The Book of Common Prayer and Administration of the Sacraments and Other Rites and Ceremonies of the Church* (Oxford University Press, 1990), 360. 2. Matt. 6:10.

Death stalks
the frail and vulnerable.
The innocent
are trampled by the strong.
Our sons and daughters
are fed to the fires of Hinnom.[3]

*Forgive me for what I have done
and left undone.*

May I not turn a blind eye to evil.
May my heart not faint
in the face of injustice.

By the power of Your Spirit within me,
may I be
unafraid,
unintimidated,
unshakable—
ready to walk into flames
to save the weak,
with no thought for my own life.

May I be bold
in faith,
in trust,
in confidence,
for such a time as this.[4]

Amen.

3. Jer. 7:31. 4. Esther 4:14.

PROVERBS 24:13–14, 16

MAY I RISE AGAIN

Lord,
despite my brave face,
I am not as strong as I pretend to be.

In times of struggle,
when I am weighed down by
worry,
failure,
loss,
my spirit falters.[1]

Though I fall,
I will rise again,
in strength.

Before the waking of the sun,
when the promise of the day
is sure to bring troubles
sufficient for its hours,
my heart wrestles.

Though I fall,
I will rise again,
in confidence.

May wisdom
illumine my coming and going,
enlighten my countenance,
dispel my fractiousness—

1. Prov. 24:10.

for I see dimly,
but one day face to face.[2]

Though I fall,
I will rise again,
in worship.

For I am hard-pressed
but not crushed;
perplexed
but not despairing;
persecuted
but not forsaken;
struck down
but not destroyed.[3]

For in all these things
I am more than a conqueror
through the One who loves me.[4]

Amen.

2. 1 Cor. 13:12. 3. 2 Cor. 4:8–9. 4. Rom. 8:37.

PROVERBS 24:28–29

VOICE OF LIGHT AND TRUTH

Father God,
blind to my own weakness,
I have stumbled through my days
grasping for acclaim,
clamoring for recognition—
a slave to the approval of others.

Forgive me,
for You alone are worthy to receive
glory,
honor,
power.[1]

Desperate for adoration,
starved for praise,
I have resorted to
arrogance,
bitterness,
superiority,
treating others as fools
to bolster my own insecurity.

Forgive me,
for from You
and through You

1. Rev. 4:11.

and to You
are all things.[2]

In my vanity,
I have embraced offense,
expecting from others
what I am unwilling to give myself.

Forgive me, Lord—
for none is righteous,
not one.[3]

I will not debase another
with lips meant for praise;
in humility
I will recognize my own sin,
as I forgive those who have sinned against me[4]—
that I may be a voice of
light and truth.

Amen.

2. Rom. 11:36. 3. Rom. 3:10–12. 4. Matt. 6:12.

PROVERBS 24:30-34

GOOD STEWARD

Father,
I long to be a good steward
of Your good gifts,
to grow in true wealth of
heart,
mind,
body,
spirit.

But I am given to waste—
time,
affection,
love—
with reckless disregard.

I see the years
slip away—
spent,
unredeemed,
for want of care.

Why squander seed
when its planting
will yield
thirty,
sixty,
a hundredfold
what was sown?[1]

1. Matt. 13:23.

To be a wise caretaker
of Your
provisions,
opportunities,
promises,
purposes
brings liberation to the soul,
light to the eyes.

Blessed Trinity,
I rise this day
in the strength of Your presence[2]—
my heart at attention,
my mind fixed upon You.[3]

By Your grace,
may I be wise,
making the best use of the time
in the midst of evil days.[4]

By Your grace,
may I waste not a moment.

Amen.

2. This line resonates with "St. Patrick's Breastplate" (*Lorica*) of the Irish prayer tradition. 3. Ps. 141:8. 4. Eph. 5:15–16.

PROVERBS 25:2

HIDDEN MYSTERIES

Lord,
I live to seek out Your ways,
to journey with You into the secret places,
to fall headlong into the mystery of Your love.

High heaven waits for those who
search out the sacred impossible,
believe the holy unimaginable,
revel in the riches of
Your wisdom and knowledge
hidden in Christ.[1]

Wrought like diamonds
in the depths of the earth
are the deep things of God:
veiled from before the foundation of the world,
the treasure of the diligent seeker.

Such knowledge is too high for me,
beyond the limits of my understanding,
an unattainable splendor.[2]
If not for the revelation of Your Spirit,
I would be blind to Your beauty.
If not for Your pursuing mercy,
I would be lost in my sin.

What no eye has seen,
no ear has heard,
what has never entered the human mind,

1. Col. 2:3. 2. Ps. 139:6.

You have prepared for those who love You[3]—
unbroken delight,
unspoiled splendor.

I will pursue as I have been pursued!
I will seek as I have been sought![4]

Show me what lies
behind the veil
of Your heart, Lord,
the wonder of Your will—
that I may know,
with all the saints,
what is the
length,
width,
height,
depth
of the love of Christ,
which surpasses knowledge,
that I may be filled
with all the fullness of God.[5]

Amen.

3. 1 Cor. 2:9. 4. Luke 15:3–7. 5. Eph. 3:18–19.

PROVERBS 25:6–7

THE LOW PLACE

Father God,
who are we
that You are mindful of us?

You have made us a little lower than angels,
crowned us with majesty and honor
to rule over creation.[1]

Who are You
that You would come to us—
gentle and humble in heart,[2]
cross-bearing,
thorn-crowned,
death-defeating,
Lord and Master of all?

In humility
You shared Your glory,
dwelling among us
in the form
of a servant.[3]

May I be of the same mind,[4]
choosing the low place—
the place of
self-denial,
self-offering,
self-sacrifice.

1. Ps. 8:3–6. 2. Matt. 11:29. 3. Phil. 2:7. 4. Phil. 2:5.

For those who exalt themselves
You humble;
those who humble themselves
You exalt.[5]

I am Your workmanship,
created for good works in Christ,[6]
formed into Your image
in ever-increasing degrees of glory,
born again to a living hope,
to an inheritance
imperishable,
undefiled,
unfading.[7]

If I would be great,
I must be small.
If I would be first,
I must be last.[8]
If I would follow You,
I must die with You.
If I would save my life,
I must lose it.[9]

May I choose the low place—
for Your power,
Your kingdom,
Your rule.

Amen.

5. Matt. 23:12. 6. Eph. 2:10. 7. 1 Pet. 1:3–4. 8. Matt. 20:25–27.
9. Matt. 16:24–25.

PROVERBS 25:11–13

A TIMELY WORD

Lord,
Your Word is life;[1]
may my lips
proclaim Your truth,
extol Your praise,
declare Your goodness.

As rain and snow grace the earth,
drawing life from the deep,
so does Your Word that goes out from Your mouth.[2]

Remind me, Lord,
that a timely word
silences fear,
binds wounds,
heals the crushed spirit.

Your Word will not return void
but will accomplish all that You intend.[3]

Remind me, Lord,
that a caring word is
a hand in the dark,
a faithful presence,
a whispered solace.

In good time, we will know joy again.
We will be led forth in peace.
The mountains and the hills shall resound with singing.[4]

1. John 6:63. 2. Isa. 55:10–11. 3. Isa. 55:11. 4. Isa. 55:12.

Remind me, Lord,
that a prayerful word
lifts burdens,
lifts sails,
sets a steady course.

The grass may wither,
the flowers may fall,
but Your Word endures forever.[5]

Remind me, Lord,
that a worshipful word
rends the heavens,
wrestles darkness,
leads the way to glory.

Sanctify us by Your truth;
Your Word is truth.[6]

Remind me, Lord,
that a loving word
ravishes the soul,
frees the captive,[7]
hails the returning King.

Lord,
Your Word is life;
may my lips
proclaim Your truth,
extol Your praise,
declare Your goodness.

Amen.

5. Isa. 40:8. 6. John 17:17. 7. Luke 4:18.

PROVERBS 25:21–22

RETURN EVIL WITH GOOD

Lord,
it is a sorry truth
that those made in Your image
withhold grace from others—
reviling rather than embracing,
scorning rather than serving.

How often have we lifted
our hands in prayer,
our voices in worship,
only to turn and raise
our hands in violence,
our voices in anger?

The fear of the Lord is the beginning of wisdom.[1]

May I be one who bears
resistance with grace,
indignation with patience,
who turns the other cheek:
grace repaid for grumbling,
peace returned for blame—
that Your kingdom would come,
Your will be done.[2]

Do not repay evil with evil,
insult with insult.[3]

1. Prov. 9:10. 2. Matt. 6:10. 3. 1 Pet. 3:9.

May I be
generous in kindness,
lavish in love,
faithful in presence
that others would know the riches of Your mercy.

Love your enemies.
Do good to those who hate you.
Bless those who curse you.
Pray for those who mistreat you.[4]

Life is too fleeting to harbor hatred,
too long to cling to grudges.
Teach me, O Lord,
to love my enemies,[5]
to return evil with good.

Amen.

4. Luke 6:27–28. 5. Matt. 5:43–48.

PROVERBS 26:1–2

JUDGE US, LORD

Lord,
this world is racked by
injustice,
inequity,
imbalance.

We glorify the foolish,
mock the holy,
chase pleasure,
forsake piety.

We have swathed ourselves in comforts,
blind to our nakedness,
content in our self-deceptions.[1]

We have stolen honor from the faithful,
lauding it upon the godless.
We have blessed and consecrated the proud,
speaking derision to the humble.

Woe to those who call evil good
and good evil.[2]

Is Your judgment
not a mercy, Lord?
Is Your heavy hand
not a kindness
to right that which is wrong?

1. 2 Pet. 2:13. 2. Isa. 5:20.

Out of the breadth of Your love,
judge us, O Lord.
Purify the thoughts and intentions of our hearts,[3]
that we may be spotless and blameless before You.[4]

Begin with me.[5]

May we who have misdirected our affirmations
repent and seek healing.

May we who have been wounded by sin
find lavish grace in our time of need.[6]

For the beauty of our flourishing,
for Your kingdom
and Your glory,
confirm us,
restore us,
strengthen us,[7]
establish us.

Amen.

3. Heb. 4:12. 4. 2 Pet. 3:14. 5. 1 Pet. 4:17–19. 6. Heb. 4:16. 7. 1 Pet. 5:10.

PROVERBS 27:1

TOMORROW

Father God,
tomorrow is a story known by You alone.
Whatever may come,
Your goodness and mercy will follow me—
for my days are numbered
by the Lover of My Soul.

By the power of Your Spirit,
may I live in the here and now—
moment by moment,
step by step,
present to Your presence with me.

In my weakness,
I look ahead to an unrealized future,
defining the worth of this day
by the potential of tomorrow.

So often I am lost in time,
wasting the sunlit hours
in fear and worry,
forsaking the gifts of Your hand.

You have given us a spirit not of fear
but of power,
love,
a sound mind.[1]

1. 2 Tim. 1:7.

Help me, Lord,
to be unanxious about the future—
for what will I gain for my worry?
These fearful thoughts add not an hour to my life.[2]

May I walk carefully,
discern wisely,
make the most of the moments I have been given,
the opportunities of the present—
for the days are evil.[3]

Fill me with gratitude today for
Your innumerable blessings,
Your sheltering mercy,
Your endless grace.[4]

Father God,
tomorrow is a story known by You alone.
Whatever may come,
Your goodness and mercy will follow me—
for my days are numbered
by the Lover of My Soul.

Amen.

2. Luke 12:25. 3. Eph. 5:15–16. 4. Ryan Whitaker Smith and Dan Wilt, *Endless Grace: Prayers Inspired by the Psalms* (Brazos, 2023), 238.

PROVERBS 27:5–6

STRONG TIES

Lord,
in my weakness I have withheld truth
for fear of rejection,
suppressed hard talk
for fear of losing a friend.

Are these bonds of brotherhood so weak?
Are these unions of flesh and blood so brittle?

By Your grace
may we put off falsehood,
speak truth to one another—
for we are members of Your body.[1]

May I be a soul of strong ties—
one who embraces admonishment,
who welcomes correction,[2]
who encourages others,
who builds others up.[3]

May I be a soul of strong ties—
one who faithfully speaks truth,
who gives generously,
who is devoted to others in love,
who honors others above myself.[4]

May I be a soul of strong ties—
weighing my words
and actions with love,

1. Eph. 4:25. 2. Prov. 27:5–6. 3. 1 Thess. 5:11. 4. Rom. 12:10.

bearing the wounds of suffering
for Your name's sake.

Amen.

PROVERBS 27:17, 19, 21

CRUCIBLE OF SUFFERING

Lord,
in the crucible of suffering
I am shaped and formed:
whetstone for blade,
diamond for glass,
fire for steel.

In the company of the saints,
I go from strength to strength[1]—
encouraged and edified[2]
by the fellowship of the holy.

In trial,
virtue is tested.
In pain,
the spirit is fortified.
In endurance,
I am made resilient.
In weakness,
I am made strong.[3]

May my heart be pure before You,[4]
my motives blameless,
my actions noble.

May I triumph in trouble—
knowing that trouble produces endurance,
endurance produces character,
character produces hope.[5]

1. Ps. 84:7. 2. 1 Thess. 5:11. 3. 2 Cor. 12:9. 4. Matt. 5:8. 5. Rom. 5:3–4.

When temptation knocks on my door,
may I be found faithful,
hoping and trusting in You alone.

Indeed, may I rejoice in the midst of trials,
knowing that in the testing of my faith[6]
I am suffering with Christ,[7]
outwardly wasting away
but inwardly renewed,
day by day—
for the troubles of this passing hour
prepare me for an eternal glory beyond compare.[8]

My longing is to know You, Lord:
the power of Your resurrection,
the fellowship of Your suffering—
that I may attain the resurrection from the dead
and find life everlasting.[9]

Amen.

6. James 1:2–3. 7. 1 Pet. 4:13. 8. 2 Cor. 4:16–17. 9. Phil. 3:10–11.

PROVERBS 28:1

FACE MY FEAR

Lord,
I know that a fear unnamed,
a foe unfaced,
can shackle the soul,
break the will.

In my worst moments,
I have run from even the notion of trouble—
making myself sick
in anticipation of an uncertain future,
crippled with worry
at the possibility of trouble.

Without
risk,
courage,
adventure,
belief in the impossible,
I am a slave to my fear—
a fragile soul fettered to despair,
taunted by voices in the night.

The Lord is
my light,
my salvation.
Whom shall I fear?[1]

Grant me the strength to walk boldly
into the Gethsemane before me:
facing affliction with resolve,

1. Ps. 27:1.

tribulation with hope,
entrusting my future to Your good grace—
Your will be done
and not my own.[2]

If You are with me,
what can come between us?[3]

Anguish?
Calamity?
Persecution?
Famine?
Nakedness?
Danger?
Death?[4]

Are You not with me
even in the darkest valley?[5]

Is Your love not stronger than
death,
life,
angels,
principalities,
the present,
the future,
powers,
height,
depth,
and all else in creation?[6]

Have You not redeemed me?
Summoned me by name?[7]
Rejoiced over me with singing?[8]

2. Matt. 26:42. 3. Rom. 8:31. 4. Rom. 8:35. 5. Ps. 23:4. 6. Rom. 8:38–39.
7. Isa. 43:1. 8. Zeph. 3:17.

Help me, O Lord,
to run this race with steadfastness,
eyes fixed upon Jesus,
who endured
suffering,
affliction,
pain,
abandonment,
for the joy set before Him.[9]

May I be resilient in the face of fear,
steadfast in my courage.

May I be faithful in the face of fear,
prolific in my praise.

May I be bold in the face of fear,
strengthened by Your presence.

Let no lord rule me
but the Lord of Heaven and Earth;
Your rod and Your staff
alone guide me,
comfort me.[10]

You are my refuge,
my strength,
my ever-present help.[11]
Never will You leave me
or forsake me[12]—
for I am Your beloved.

Amen.

9. Heb. 12:1–2. 10. Ps. 23:4. 11. Ps. 46:1. 12. Deut. 31:8.

PROVERBS 28:5

YOUR JUSTICE

The wise seek justice.
Justice seeks the wise.

If I am unwilling to fight for those in need,
who will fight for me in my hour of trial?

To stand up for the vulnerable[1]
is to see You in the eyes of the oppressed;
to shatter the bonds of oppression,
to loose the captives,[2]
is to invite Your kingdom to come
on this broken earth.

If our justice lacks
love,
empathy,
kindness,
if it does not
heal the brokenhearted,
proclaim freedom,
heal blindness,
it is not Your justice.[3]

May we walk in humility,
knowing none is righteous,[4]
but all fall short of Your glory.[5]

Your justice,
administered by the

1. Ps. 82:3. 2. Luke 4:18–19. 3. Luke 4:18. 4. Rom. 3:10. 5. Rom. 3:23.

Weigher of Hearts,
Balancer of Scales,
Seeker of Our Good,
is a justice wed to hope,
leading to
wholeness,
mercy,
forgiveness,
restitution,
redemption,
drawing all with ears to hear,
eyes to see
to the freedom of Your presence.

You have shown me
what is good and what You require—
to walk in step with You
in the light of Your goodness,
to bear the fruit of Your kingdom
all the days of my life.[6]

May my heart be pure,
my hands be clean,
my will be surrendered,
my mind be wed to wisdom,
as I follow the leading of Your Spirit
and seek to do Your will.

You are the Just Judge, O Lord.
Righteousness and justice
are the foundation of Your throne.
Steadfast love and faithfulness
go before You.[7]

6. Ps. 23:6. 7. Ps. 89:14.

PROVERBS 28:13–14

I CONFESS

"Neither do I condemn you;
go and sin no more."[1]

In Your words,
Lord and Christ,
I find strength for my confession:

Against You
and You alone
have I sinned.[2]
Have mercy on me, O God,
for Your love extends to the heavens.[3]
Remove my transgressions;
cleanse me from evil's stain.
You know me,
inside and out;
nothing escapes You.[4]
I have been sin-bent
since my eyes first caught light.
You desire faithfulness in the heart,
wisdom within the spirit.[5]
Cleanse me with hyssop,
and I will be clean;
wash me white as snow.[6]
Listen, my soul, for joy!
Mend all that is broken, for life!
Be gone, iniquity![7]

1. John 8:11. 2. Ps. 51:4. 3. Ps. 51:1. 4. Ps. 51:3–4. 5. Ps. 51:5–6. 6. Ps. 51:7. 7. Ps. 51:8–9.

Take root, purity!
Be steadfast, my spirit!
May I walk in intimacy with You, Lord,
as Your Good Spirit
tends to me.
Make me a willing soul
for the long road ahead,[8]
instructing others
in the ways of Your goodness,
welcoming all wanderers home.[9]

Hear my confession.
Extend to me Your mercy.

Nothing is hidden from Your sight;
to You every tangled heart is laid bare.[10]

I acknowledge my sin,
that the truth may set me free,[11]
that divine absolution
may cleanse me.[12]

It is my yielded spirit,
my contrite heart,[13]
that pleases You,
my obedience and love,[14]
rather than my sacrifices,
that blesses You.

My ears had heard of You;
now my eyes have seen You.[15]
You know all things.
Your purposes are unfading.[16]

8. Ps. 51:10–12. 9. Ps. 51:13. 10. Heb. 4:13. 11. John 8:32. 12. Ps. 51:10. 13. Ps. 51:16–17. 14. 1 Sam. 15:22; John 14:15. 15. Job 42:5. 16. Job 42:2.

As for me,
I have spoken of matters
beyond my comprehension,
obscured true knowledge
in my quest for enlightenment.[17]

Lord and Christ,
teach me the way of repentance—
of submission,
attention,
silence,
surrender.[18]

In confession lies my salvation:
to look,
unflinching,
upon my own brokenness;
to receive a grace unearned,
a mercy undeserved.
Such knowledge is too wonderful for me[19]—
I am loved beyond imagining.[20]

By Your strength, Lord,
may I go and sin no more.

For repentance is wisdom.

In the name of Jesus,
Amen.

17. Job 42:3. 18. Job 42:1–6. 19. Ps. 139:6. 20. Eph. 3:14–21.

PROVERBS 29:1

GENTLENESS AND HUMILITY

Choose the way of
gentleness and humility,[1]
and lower yourself,[2]
my soul.

Choose the way of
gentleness and humility,
and welcome guidance,
my soul.

Choose the way of
gentleness and humility,
and invite the Spirit,
my soul.

Choose the way of
gentleness and humility,
and embrace hiddenness,
my soul.

Choose the way of
gentleness and humility,
and resist the devil,[3]
my soul.

Choose the way of
gentleness and humility,
and deny pride,
my soul.

1. Matt. 11:29. 2. James 4:10. 3. James 4:7.

Choose the way of
gentleness and humility,
and empty yourself—
make yourself nothing,
take on the form of a servant[4]—
cling to this posture of heart,
that your spirit may be prepared
for eternity.

Those who exalt themselves will be humbled.
Those who humble themselves will be exalted.[5]

Lord God,
I lie before You,
facedown
on holy ground,
that I might find rest for my soul[6]—
for You are near to the humble
and contrite in spirit.[7]

I choose the way of
gentleness and humility—
You are gentle and humble in heart,
and in You there is rest for all who are weary.[8]

May Your way
become my way—
for where else would I go?
You have the words of life.[9]

Amen.

4. Phil. 2:1–11. 5. Matt. 23:12. 6. Matt. 11:29. 7. Isa. 66:2. 8. Matt. 11:29.
9. John 6:68.

PROVERBS 29:13

LIGHT TO THE EYES OF ALL

Living as equals—
alike in dignity,
alike in majesty—
I move among those made in Your image.[1]

We are
interconnected,
intertwined,
interrelated,
called to Your high purpose,
fashioned for New Creation.

And yet we harm one another,
seeking our own gain—
the oppressor
and the oppressed,
the captor
and the captive.

You give light to the eyes of all.
The rain falls on the just and unjust alike.[2]
You store up mercy for all who turn to You.
In Your house are many rooms.[3]

Sin taints every bond—
disconnects,
disentwines,

1. Gen. 1:27. 2. Matt. 5:45. 3. John 14:2.

isolates
us from one another.

Brother reviles brother.
Sister disdains sister.
Pride is a chasm between us.

In Your mercy,
intervene for us:
bring unity where there is discord,
healing where there is wounding.

By the power of Your Holy Spirit,
may we be
bridge builders,
agents of peace,
Your hands and feet in a hurting world,[4]
proclaiming the reconciling truth
of Your Gospel.[5]

You give light to the eyes of all.
The rain falls on the just and unjust alike.
You store up mercy for all who turn to You.
In Your house are many rooms.

4. Eph. 2:10. 5. 2 Cor. 5:18.

PROVERBS 29:18

RESTORE MY VISION

Jesus,
to behold You as You are,
in all Your splendor and glory,[1]
is vision enough
for a lifetime.

Restore my vision—
that I may drink of the water of life
and never thirst again.

Restore my vision—
that my soul may feast on the Bread of Life
and never hunger again.

You are the bread from heaven.[2]
Your body is true food,
Your blood true drink.[3]

Restore my vision—
that I may not perish
but pass from death to life.

Restore my vision—
that I may walk faithfully with You:
delighting in Your presence,
abounding in joy and peace.

I was buried with You
that I may be raised with You.

1. Ps. 63:2. 2. John 6:32. 3. John 6:55.

I died with You
that I may live with You.[4]

Restore my vision—
that confusion may be dispelled,
fear released,
faith fanned into flame.[5]

Restore my vision—
that the eyes of my heart would be enlightened
to behold You,
Light of the world,[6]
as You are,
as I long for the day
when I will look upon Your face
in unhindered glory.[7]

In that day,
I will know
as I have been known.[8]
My heart will rejoice.
My joy will be full.
And I will ask nothing more of You.[9]

Amen.

4. Rom. 6:8. 5. 2 Tim. 1:6. 6. John 8:12. 7. 1 Cor. 13:12. 8. 1 Cor. 13:12. 9. John 16:22–23.

PROVERBS 30:24–31

LEAD US

Your gifts, O God, are many.
To each is given a manifestation of the Spirit—
for the good of us all.[1]

The wise
lead with godly insight,
words seasoned with salt.

Lead us—
with humility.

The leaders
lead with holy grit
and heroism of spirit.

Lead us—
with courage.

The organizers
lead with boldness
and godly ingenuity.

Lead us—
with clarity.

The lovers lead
with sonnets of the heart,
a poetry of compassion.

1. 1 Cor. 12:7.

Lead us—
with love.

The shepherds lead
with tender guidance
and heavenly insight.

Lead us—
with care.

The faith-filled lead
with songs of hope
and shouts of deliverance.

Lead us—
with joy.

The prophets lead
with eternal vision
and edifying mystery.

Lead us—
with wonder.

The artists lead
with transcendent beauty,
the stirring of the heart.

Lead us—
with delight.

Christ, lead us,
as all creation proclaims Your glory.

Amen.

PROVERBS 31:8–9

MY VOICE

Lord,
I have a voice—
a voice You have given me.

May the words of my mouth,
the meditation of my heart,
be pleasing to You.[1]

I will use my voice
to plead for more than my own rights—
defending the oppressed,
the fatherless,
the widow.[2]

I will use my voice
to champion more than my own security—
to loose chains of injustice,
to break yokes of bondage.[3]

I will use my voice
to provide for more than my own family—
to share my food with the hungry,
to shelter the wanderer,
to clothe the naked.[4]

Will my light not then break forth like the dawn?[5]
My night become as noonday?[6]
Will righteousness not go before me,
Your glory pursue me?[7]

1. Ps. 19:14. 2. Isa. 1:17. 3. Isa. 58:6. 4. Isa. 58:7. 5. Isa. 58:8. 6. Isa. 58:10. 7. Isa. 58:8.

I have a voice—
a voice You have given me.

I will use it to praise You,[8]
to bless Your name while I have breath,[9]
to lift my fellow sojourners
along this winding road to glory.[10]

Amen.

8. Ps. 18:49. 9. Ps. 63:4. 10. Matt. 7:14.

PROVERBS 31:10–12, 30

A BLESSING FOR THE SISTERS

Lord of All Blessings,
I thank You for the sisters—
faithful and true;[1]
yielded to Your love,
carrying the weight of the world
upon their shoulders,
new life within their arms.

The sisters display Your beauty:
radiant with light;[2]
reflecting Your kindness
as they nurture and guide,
nourish and sustain,
lead with grace and wisdom.

They are fierce in love,
impassioned by faith;
interceding for nations,[3]
lifting the burdens of others.

They are generous
in truth and compassion;[4]
walking humbly,
heart to heart with the Spirit.[5]

1. Luke 18:8. 2. Phil. 2:15. 3. Ps. 2:8. 4. Col. 3:12. 5. Eph. 6:18.

Hear my cry, O Lord,
attend to my prayer[6]
for such a time as this:[7]

We pray for the sisters.

May they become
women of godly countenance—
encouraged,
helped,
inspired,
renewed,
transformed,
delighted,
empowered,
supported.

May they become
models of
resilience,
leadership,
compassion,
respect,
awareness,
prayer,
innovation,
faith.

May they become
recipients of
grace,
mercy,
kindness,

6. Ps. 61:1. 7. Esther 4:14.

hospitality,
opportunity,
companionship,
resources,
trust.

May they become
the best of
friends,
confidants,
givers,
receivers,
leaders,
adventurers,
companions,
saints.

May every daughter in the house of God
come into the full fruition
of her high and holy calling—
strong as Mary,[8]
courageous as Esther,[9]
loyal as Ruth.[10]

May each sister rise in faithful obedience,
for wisdom begins in knowing You—
beat of Your heart,
bend of Your will,[11]
beauty of Your holiness,[12]
brightness of Your Word.[13]

Amen.

8. Luke 1:38. 9. Esther 4:15. 10. Ruth 1:16–17. 11. Matt. 12:50. 12. Ps. 96:9. 13. Ps. 119:105.

ACKNOWLEDGMENTS

The prayers in this book were written in homes, offices, coffee shops, and other miscellaneous locations both domestic and abroad, including Nashville, Los Angeles, Santa Fe, Budapest, and London, to name just a few. For all the places that made us feel at home throughout the process, we are grateful. A special thanks to Bob Hosack and the entire team at Brazos Press for their continued belief in these books. To our spouses, our children, our friends—you were the first to read early drafts of a handful of "prayers inspired by the Scriptures" nearly five years ago, which set this whole adventure on its course. Your ongoing encouragement has meant more than you could possibly know.